THE TECHNOLOGY TRAP

Science and the Military

Other AFA Books

FRISBEE
Makers of the United States Air Force

MROZEK
Air Power and the Ground War in Vietnam

SMITH
Assignment Pentagon—The Insider's Guide

WARDEN
The Air Campaign: Planning for Combat

Other AUSA Books

GALVIN
The Minute Men: The First Flight—Myths and Realities of the American Revolution

MATTHEWS and BROWN
The Challenge of Military Leadership

MATTHEWS and BROWN
The Parameters of Military Ethics

SMITH
Assignment Pentagon—The Insider's Guide

Titles of related interest from Brassey's

HARTCUP
The War of Invention

JAMES
Imperial Rearguard

LEE et al
Guided Weapons

POWELL and FORREST
Noise in the Military Environment

TILL
Modern Sea Power

GATES and LYNN
Ships, Submarines and the Sea

MASON
Air Power

WALKER
Air-to-Ground Operations

Related Periodicals*

Armed Forces Journal International
Defense Analysis
Middle East Strategic Studies Quarterly
Survival

* Specimen copies available upon request.

AN AFA BOOK   AN AUSA BOOK

THE TECHNOLOGY TRAP

Science and the Military

TIMOTHY GARDEN

*Published in the United States
of America in association with*

*the Aerospace Education Foundation
Air Force Association*

*the Institute of Land Warfare
Association of the U.S. Army*

BRASSEY'S DEFENCE PUBLISHERS

(A member of the Maxwell Pergamon Publishing Corporation)

LONDON · OXFORD · WASHINGTON · NEW YORK · BEIJING
FRANKFURT · SÃO PAULO · SYDNEY · TOKYO · TORONTO

U
42
.G37
1989

UK (Editorial)	Brassey's Defence Publishers Ltd., 24 Gray's Inn Road, London WC1X 8HR, England
(Orders)	Brassey's Defence Publishers Ltd., Headington Hill Hall, Oxford OX3 0BW, England
USA (Editorial)	Pergamon–Brassey's International Defense Publishers, Inc., 8000 Westpark Drive, Fourth Floor, McLean, Virginia 22102, U.S.A.
(Orders)	Pergamon Press, Inc., Maxwell House, Fairview Park, Elmsford, New York 10523, U.S.A.
PEOPLE'S REPUBLIC OF CHINA	Pergamon Press, Room 4037, Qianmen Hotel, Beijing, People's Republic of China
FEDERAL REPUBLIC OF GERMANY	Pergamon Press GmbH, Hammerweg 6, D-6242 Kronberg, Federal Republic of Germany
BRAZIL	Pergamon Editora Ltda, Rua Eça de Queiros, 346, CEP 04011, Paraiso, São Paulo, Brazil
AUSTRALIA	Pergamon–Brassey's Defence Publishers Pty Ltd., P.O. Box 544, Potts Point, N.S.W. 2011, Australia
JAPAN	Pergamon Press, 5th Floor, Matsuoka Central Building, 1-7-1 Nishishinjuku, Shinjuku-ku, Tokyo 160, Japan
CANADA	Pergamon Press Canada Ltd., Suite No 271, 253 College Street, Toronto, Ontario, Canada M5T 1R5

Copyright © 1989 Brassey's Defence Publishers Ltd

First edition 1989

Library of Congress Cataloging in Publication Data
Garden, Timothy.
The technology trap : science and the military / Timothy Garden. – 1st ed.
p.   cm.
Bibliography: p.
1. Military art and science—History—20th century.
2. High technology.   3. Technology and state.
4. Science and state.
I. Title.
U42.G37 1989   355'.07—dc19   88-37058

British Library Cataloguing in Publication Data
Garden, Timothy
The technology trap: science and the military
1. Warfare. Technological innovation
I. Title
355'.02

ISBN 0 08 036710-0
ISBN 0 08 037690-8 US Edition

Printed in Great Britain by BPCC Wheatons Ltd., Exeter

An AUSA Institute of Land Warfare Book

THE ASSOCIATION OF THE UNITED STATES ARMY, or AUSA, was founded in 1950 as a not-for-profit organization dedicated to education concerning the role of the U.S. Army, to providing material for military professional development, and to the promotion of proper recognition and appreciation of the profession of arms. Its constituencies include those who serve in the Army today, including Army National Guard, Army Reserve, and Army civilians, and the retirees and veterans who have served in the past, and all their families. A large number of public-minded citizens and business leaders are also an important constituency. The Association seeks to educate the public, elected and appointed officials, and leaders of defense industry on crucial issues involving the adequacy of our national defense, particularly those issues affecting land warfare.

In 1988 AUSA established within its existing organization a new entity known as the Institute of Land Warfare. Its purpose is to extend the educational work of AUSA by sponsoring scholarly publications, to include books, monographs, and essays on key defense issues, as well as workshops and symposia. Among the volumes chosen for designation as "An AUSA Institute of Land Warfare Book" are both new texts and reprints of titles of enduring value that are no longer in print. Topics include history, policy issues, strategy, and tactics. Publication as an AUSA Book does not indicate that the Association of the United States Army and the publisher agree with everything in the book, but does suggest that the AUSA and the publisher believe this book will stimulate the thinking of AUSA members and others concerned about important issues.

An AFA/AEF Book

THE AIR FORCE ASSOCIATION (AFA), established on February 6, 1946, is an independent veterans' organization whose objective is to promote greater understanding of aerospace and national defense issues. On May 1, 1956, AFA established the Aerospace Education Foundation (AEF). The Foundation was established as a nonprofit organization in order to formulate and administer AFA's educational outreach programs.

With a membership of more than 240,000, AFA represents all elements of the Air Force family, military and civilian, active and retired, Reserve and National Guard, cadet and veteran, Civil Air Patrol, civil service, and aerospace workers.

Pergamon-Brassey's AFA Book Series is designed to assist AFA's Aerospace Education Foundation in fulfilling its mandate. AEF's goal is to inform AFA members—and indeed anyone involved in the national defense dialogue—about issues vital to the future of the U.S. Air Force in particular and air power in general. Forthcoming AFA Books may cover the topics of aerospace history, biography, technology, combat, strategy and tactics, personnel, management, leadership, and policy. Publication as an AFA Book does not indicate that the Air Force Association and the publisher agree with everything in the book, but does suggest that the AFA and the publisher believe this book will stimulate the thinking of AFA members and others concerned about important issues.

To Sue, Alex and Antonia

Contents

Preface

THIS BOOK has been over three years in preparation, partly because of the range of topics to be covered, and partly because of the more pressing calls on the time of a serving officer. Indeed, my first thoughts for a volume about the impact of technology on warfare date back even further to an air power conference in 1982. While much that was said there was ephemeral, it was something said by the late Jonathan Alford which started me thinking. In an aphorism worthy of Oscar Wilde, he explained that 'technology always delivers less, arrives later and costs more than forecast'. This cynical view struck a chord with many of the military men in his audience. Certainly to this military man, the money wasted on developing capabilities which never see operational service has appeared to be a recurrent tragedy.

This book does not seek to find the reasons for past failures, nor is it a parochial reflection of what might have been, or might yet be, in British defence policy. Rather I have examined the importance of science to the military in the past, and attempted to draw out some common threads for the future. Modern science will offer the possibility of many new weapon systems both to us and to our potential adversaries. In this book, I have indicated some of the more significant areas, which could influence warfare over the next thirty years.

The progress in research in the different sciences is culled from the open literature, and its application is either already documented or the product of my fertile imagination. Certainly, suggestions that particular research might have military applications does not mean that any nation will necessarily follow my suggested path. Indeed some of the ideas explored appear to lead down blind alleys, where security is not enhanced after much money has been spent. By a broad review of the possibilities, and as importantly the limitations, I hope to give the reader a greater appreciation for the difficulties we face. Technology is expensive and defence resources everywhere are limited; choices must, therefore, be made. It appears that some areas—such as anti-satellite weapons—offer better returns than others. We also face greater risks from some developments, such as the next generation of chemical and biological warfare agents.

What each nation decides as its priorities will depend on many factors, and I do not presume to advise. However, all who are involved in influencing the decision-making process, either from inside or without, have a duty to understand the capabilities and limitations of modern science. Much is claimed by those with vested interests but, unless proper objective analysis is carried out, we are likely to repeat the mistakes of the past. These mistakes have been both to miss opportunities for new breakthroughs, and also to invest in technologies which offered no improvement in security.

I am grateful to my colleagues of all three Services and of the academic strategic studies community, who offered advice and criticism. The results remain entirely my own, and in no way reflect any official thinking or policy.

London   TIMOTHY GARDEN
January 1989

CHAPTER 1

Technology and Military Power

THE advances of technology in the twentieth century have been revolutionary in their impact on every nation. We can travel throughout the world in a matter of hours. We can communicate virtually instantaneously with anyone, wherever they may be. Complex machines are manufactured automatically, and made from materials which are unknown in nature. Behind all these tangible effects is the deeper understanding of the nature of matter which the physicists, chemists, biologists and mathematicians have given us through the fruits of pure science research. At the same time this technological progress has given us the nuclear warhead, the inter-continental ballistic missile, biological and chemical warfare agents, precision-guided munitions, supersonic jet bombers, nuclear-powered submarines and an endless choice of killing systems for conducting war. The pace of technological innovation shows no signs of slackening. An optimist would hope that the future enhancements in both communications and wealth-producing capacity would offer the prospect of a future of global harmony, with no competition for resources, territory or power. At the same time, the remorseless progress in military scientific achievement offers an increasing range of more effective ways to wage war; and it does so to an ever greater number of nations and terrorist organizations.

It is beyond the scope of this book to examine the global benefits that technology may provide tomorrow. It is to be hoped that global communication will improve understanding, increasing productivity will raise living standards everywhere, and that renewable energy sources and new materials will reduce dependence on strategic resources. Such a rosy technological future should allow more harmonious international relations to develop, yet current trends point to a more pessimistic prospect being equally valid. The ability to threaten other nations' vital interests from great distances, the imbalance between rich and poor nations being worsened by a technology gap, and the divergence of political systems all suggest that security and peace will need to be earned in the future, just as they have had to be in the past.

1

In subsequent Chapters we examine how technology affects the maintenance of peace and security. First, the key developments of the past are highlighted in each of the military specializations. Then, the potential of each of the major areas of scientific interest is reviewed. Finally, the possibilities for the future of warfare are explored. The influence of technology on warfare is not a new concern. As each development in weapon design has been made, some new response has been stimulated to act as a counter to the new capability. It is often suggested that today the nature of the problem is changing.

In the past, developments have, for the most part, been incremental in nature. The significant breakthroughs such as aircraft, submarine, machine-gun, tank, missile and atomic bomb have taken years to come to fruition and full deployment. Now we are told that technology is leaping ahead in every research field: high energy physics, computing, nuclear physics, space, chemistry, materials, biotechnology, and electronics. Not only are all these fields experiencing new discoveries at rates which appear exponential, but the rate of innovation in the military sphere is faster than the production and development cycle can cope with. Thus new weapons become based on obsolete technology before they enter operational service.

There are those who advocate comprehensive military research into each and every new technological avenue of interest. It is argued that to ignore the possibilities may open a new vulnerability, given that potential adversaries may gain a decisive breakthrough in a critical research area. Such a massive commitment could only be achieved at enormous cost in both financial and scientific resources. As is shown later in this volume, many of the most exciting research areas need vast investment over a long period. The research scientists are themselves a finite resource and, if used in one area, are unavailable for other work in either the civil or military areas. For most nations, it will be necessary to allocate priorities on the best assessment of the balance of risk against the financial and resource burden. Limitations on money available for research, development and procurement of high technology military equipment mean that choices must be made as to which option to pursue. Yet these choices, by their very nature, have to be made on limited knowledge and dubious extrapolation. If a development is to be innovative and dependent on novel techniques, its costs, effectiveness and timescale for production can only be speculative. Yet the choices which are made on such a basis will have profound long term effects on the force structures of the nation, its economic strength and, ultimately, on its security.

While these problems beset governments of both big and small nations, the greatest technological impact on military forces is seen in NATO and the Warsaw Pact. The West has enjoyed an advantage in innovation through commercial research, freedom within the academic community and growing wealth. As a result, NATO nations have looked increasingly for technological solutions to their concerns over the adverse balance of forces with the Warsaw Pact. If advantage could be bought through such innovation, then the price would be worth paying. If too many resources are wasted on non-productive technology, then such an approach could increase vulnerability. The West spends large amounts on a range of military research projects, some of which may be successful and lead to new capabilities and others which will not. An alternative strategy, which many believe the Soviet Union has adopted, is to steal the fruits of the opponent's research. It can wait to see which areas are fruitful, import the technology clandestinely or, in some cases, as open commercial purchases and then devote greater resources to the deployment of large numbers of the new and more effective systems. It is for this reason that the United States has taken such a strong line on technology transfer in recent years. Such methods are not new, nor have they been exclusively the province of the Soviet Union.

What then is the optimum strategy for technology and military systems? It is not possible simply to ignore what technology can offer, and depend on resources devoted to increasingly obsolete equipment. To do so would be to court disaster. The military balance is a dynamic equation in which quantity and quality of men and weapons are interdependent factors. While analysis of set piece battles brought early operational researchers to the view that quantity was of greater significance (that you needed four times the combat capability to match a doubling of enemy size), present day wargamers look for much better returns from technology. In theory, we could produce a large squadron of World War II bombers for the price of a Tornado aircraft today. Yet not a single one could survive to reach the target in a modern air defence environment. The accuracy and all-weather capability of today's aircraft makes it worth that squadron of Lancasters in effectiveness. But if all the resources are placed in just one aircraft then, however effective it may be, a single bullet may be sufficient to destroy the force. This is the basis of the concern over the road to absurdity, as each generation of new military equipment is more capable, but less numerous. If the trend is not broken, a time will come when nations will be unable to afford more than one aircraft.

The question is not one of whether technology can offer improvements in military capability—of that there is no doubt. The key issue is, with limited resources, how can the technologies which offer the greatest promise for military use be exploited, and hence increase national security. This is a difficult problem, and any analysis must depend on assumptions about the nature of the future threat, the prospects of technological progress in particular areas, the character of international relations, national and global economic prospects, and a host of unquantifiable social and political factors. Potential enemies must make similar decisions, and the technologies they opt for will influence the effort needed on research for countermeasures.

To make a rational allocation of priorities for research effort requires an assessment of the relative importance of differing military roles and equipment. In the West our first concern must be the preservation of peace through deterrence; and the potential adversary is the Soviet Union and its Warsaw Pact allies. This does not discount either the emergence of other potentially hostile Great Powers, or the continuing risk of low-intensity conflicts in widely-separated regions of the world. Nor can the fact that technology will bring greater destructive capability into the hands of lesser powers be ignored. Nevertheless the catastrophic potential inherent in a superpower conflict must remain our first concern.

In the remainder of this volume, potential weapons for the superpowers are the main theme. They are not specified for one particular nation as science is of itself on no state's side. The aim is to highlight those areas which may bear fruit for whichever nation decides to invest, and then to consider what countermeasures are available to others. The greatest difficulty in a time of such scientific plenty is to preserve a sense of perspective. Today's miracle weapon is tomorrow's dead end. The next three Chapters attempt to give that sense of perspective by examining how science has affected maritime, land and air warfare in the past. The technological developments which have crucially affected the way war has been conducted over the past two centuries are described, and their common features sought. Space does not permit an examination of the many scientific novelties which came to naught, although there are many lessons for the military prophet in those disasters.

In the subsequent Chapters the major areas of current scientific research, both pure and applied, are described. Many already have military applications, some have potential for weapons, others are perhaps given too much weight in the allocation of priorities for resources. Again some—for instance the integrated circuit—have applications in nearly every form of military effort. Yet even then the cost benefits will vary with applications to different weapon types: making a tank shell 'intelligent' will have a different investment return from giving an offensive aircraft an all-weather flying performance. It would be possible to go one stage further and postulate scientific problems whose solution would change the nature of war: the negation of gravity, the elimination of radiation effects, perpetual motion, telepathy, weather control. These and other speculative concepts must rightly remain for the present in the realms of science fiction. We consider only those applications which current theory shows to be possible and have a reasonable chance of successful development, given sufficient resources and perhaps as long as two decades of development work.

In the concluding four Chapters of the book, the application of these technologies to future warfare is explored. While different nations will have different needs, the aim is to produce a menu of technical opportunities from which an appropriate selection could be made. Hardware cannot be the whole story. How that military force would be used is also crucial. The debate on tactical doctrine in the light of new technologies is only just beginning. A frequent accusation is that the military have always planned to fight the last war. The current discussions about tactical doctrine for equipment which is still in the laboratory leads one to fear that the pendulum may have swung too far the other way.

It is vital that force structures and tactical doctrine are reviewed in the light of new capabilities. Such changes should not be implemented before the capability is deployed, and should also take into account the political realities. In some cases the tactics may be constrained by the political limitations put on a new weapon system. However, if a new capability and doctrine can produce more security at less cost, then the proper assessment should influence the political constraints. There are difficulties with such assessments. Traditional combat-proven military techniques may be abandoned in a wave of enthusiasm for novel fighting tactics which work well in computer simulations, war games, exercises and theoretical studies, yet have never undergone the acid test of battle. Indeed, the problem of lack of combat experience is all-pervading for weapon designers and the military. The Vulcan nuclear bomber aircraft was so successful in its deterrent role that it was some thirty years after its designers had worked at its specifications that it was first used in anger. The conventional bombing in the Falklands conflict of May 1982 was neither a role nor a location which could possibly have been foreseen by the architects of Britain's strategic nuclear deterrent force in the 1940s.

A recurring lesson of successive conflicts has been that wars never run according to plan for either side. Contingency plans, when they exist, must be changed or scrapped; equipment must be misemployed; and improvisation and initiative become more important than firepower and technical superiority. This leads to yet another caution in any approach to novel technologies. Do they improve the versatility of the military machine? New weapon systems can be designed to be more flexible in their applications, or they can become more specialized. Worst of all, weapons can be designed around a specific contingency or scenario which today may appear likely, but in the future, or in the event of war, may come to seem tragically ridiculous.

The aim must be to invest in those areas of scientific research that offer the promise of enhanced security at an affordable price, and which leave sufficient flexibility to cope with the unforeseeable defence problems of the future. There are areas of technological advancement which carry the risk of decreasing security through a reduction in strategic stability, flexibility, cost effectiveness, political will, military forces or public support. These are fruitful areas for arms control negotiations, as it can be in no state's interest to develop capabilities which reduce its security.

In the West, the cornucopia of novel technologies has meant that we have increasingly sought a technical answer to every security concern. If we devote increasing resources to the expanding range of opportunities, we may find ourselves less and less able to afford to procure the weapons that we need for our security. This is the Technology Trap, and it has as its bait 'the neat solution'. Just like the cheese in a mousetrap, the apparently free benefit may carry a hidden and terminal cost.

Part One – Lessons from the Past

CHAPTER 2

Maritime Warfare

WAR AT sea has a long and well-documented history. Given that three-quarters of the Earth's surface is ocean, that until recently international trade has depended almost exclusively on sea transport, and that nation states have grown up around points of access to the oceans, it is scarcely surprising that control of the sea routes has assumed such strategic significance. This century has seen naval conflict extend from the two dimensional operations of surface fleets into a theatre which encompasses the space and air above the oceans, as well as the deeps beneath the surface of the sea. Technical developments have radically changed the character and method of naval warfare. To judge the elements of naval power most relevant to the future, it is worth examining those innovations which have so dramatically changed the war at sea over the past two centuries.

Since the time of the Phoenicians, naval warfare had consisted of combat between warships intent on the sinking or capture of their adversaries. In the nineteenth century the nature of the warship was revolutionized by the development of steam power. Sea power could be applied rapidly where and when it was required. It was no longer dependent on the vagaries of the wind or, in more ancient times, the strength of the oarsmen. The transition from sail to steam for fighting ships was not instantly recognized as a significant advance in the art of maritime warfare. Dating the invention of the steam-powered ship from William Symington's steamboat the *Charlotte Dundas*, in 1802, it would be another fifty-five years before the British navy finally abandoned its last sail warship. Innovation was not to be rushed in those days. It is interesting to compare it with military adoption of aircraft a century later, following the first heavier-than-air flying machine in 1903. If progress had been as slow, then balloons would be in use for offensive operations concurrently with supersonic fighter-bombers.

The vulnerabilities to gunfire of the paddle-steamer with its engine above the water line continued until the introduction of the screw propellor. Despite the idea dating from Archimedes, it was 1839 before the first major screw-driven warship was built (named after the

7

venerable Greek himself). The move to steam power was not without penalties. While the wind might not be reliable, it was at least universally available and provided free of charge. Steam power needed fuel to generate it. Ships were tied to supply lines and coaling stations, and combat radius became limited by refuelling requirements. Technology could provide ships with power on demand at the price of range limitation. The price had to be paid. The advantage gained by being able to ignore the winds far outweighed the logistic penalty. Steam power had an absolute advantage over sail, and that meant that sail warships would always be beaten in a battle against a mechanically powered warship.

In any form of fight the outcome depends on a combination of how well the fighter can defend himself against the blows of his enemy, as well as on how hard he can deliver blows. Speed and manoeuvrability were critical in both regards for warships. When under attack, powered ships could cut and run. When attacking, they could position themselves rapidly to gain the most advantageous position. Technology was also offering improvements to the defence in the form of protective materials for building ships. Iron offered much better resilience to attack than wood. As the armour plating became more efficient, naval guns were developed to have more penetrating power. In the second half of the last century there was a continual race between firepower and armour for ships. In two decades the thickness of the iron protection increased from 4.5 to 24 inches,[1] and new manufacturing processes made the armour even stronger. The technical developments were driving the increasingly rapid replacement rate for warships, each needing better armour and better guns than its predecessor. Sea power more than ever before became a reflection of a nation's industrial capability.

The critical change in the nature of sea power from sail to steam had taken the first half of the century to become incorporated into the world's navies; the incremental changes to armour and firepower were introduced with increasing rapidity. Two new devices for sinking ships affected the conduct of operations in the second half of the nineteenth century: the mine and the torpedo. Mines could be used to defend home ports, to deny access and to provide offensive firepower across expected enemy shipping routes. Primitive torpedoes saw service in the American Civil War and, over the years that followed, were developed to incorporate compressed air motors, depth control and gyroscopic steering. The significance of the torpedo was its ability to provide a threat to capital ships from small launch platforms. The torpedo boat was a relatively inexpensive way to provide potentially devastating firepower. But such boats were themselves vulnerable to specially-designed destroyers, which were built to protect the warships. The torpedo boat in turn could best be protected by hiding it under the sea, and the submarine provided the answer. From a practical demonstration by Bourgeous and Brun in 1863, France, Britain and the United States were all fielding torpedo-equipped submarines by the turn of the century.

By the start of the twentieth century, naval warfare had been transformed from the meeting of ships at close quarters for a cannon fight, a battering engagement or a boarding. The advent of more powerful and accurate guns, torpedoes from boats and submarines, and mines had made naval engagements far more complex. The warship was becoming more heavily armoured and carrying more firepower, which made it both more expensive and more attractive as a target. It needed to be protected by destroyers and mine clearance systems. While the nature of maritime warfare was changing because of technological innovation, scientific advances were being made in many fields which could have military applications: the internal combustion engine, wireless telegraphy and electricity in particular. It is not unreasonable to draw a comparison between the strategic environment of the early years of this century and the world as it is today. In both cases nations were devoting considerable resources to military equipment, the nature of war had been changed by technology, there had been little opportunity to test new systems in combat, and scientific discoveries were offering many novel opportunities for military development.

How did the world's naval powers respond to the opportunities for technological advantage? The British set the pace for bigger and bigger warships with the *Dreadnought* and subsequent giants. Smaller numbers of larger ships were forecast to be more cost-effective.[2] Thickness of armour and size and number of guns (with rotating turrets and centralized fire control) were maximized to produce very expensive capital ships. Designers, looking for cheaper ways to combat these warships, traded armour for speed and manoeuvrability in the cruisers. The French produced more submarines than the other powers, but depended on petrol-engine propulsion.

In the event, World War I had a number of surprises for maritime operations. The super battleships met rarely in combat, and spent much of the war ensuring that they were in safe havens. In the major engagement at Jutland, the heavy armour proved its worth in such set piece battles, and the cruisers suffered severely. This victory for the British fleet gave no critical strategic advantage, as control of the surface of the sea was no longer the only consideration. The day of the submarine had arrived. At the beginning of the war Germany had only ten diesel-powered U-boats and another eighteen petrol engined.[3] Yet in the opening days it was able to force the Royal Navy to move from Scapa Flow because of the threat. More importantly, the success of the submarine against merchant shipping could have been a war-winning capability. The U-boats were so effective that, had it not been for inhibitions on production and operations after American protests to the Kaiser, they might have deprived Britain of the resources to continue the war. The crucial importance of containing the submarine threat led to much effort being devoted to anti-submarine warfare technology. The hydrophone, depth-charge, anti-submarine destroyer, aircraft-spotting, and mines all contributed to the solution. With the benefit of hindsight, the historian can point to a possibly more effective scheme for defence equipment development in the early 1900s. The power of the submarine was not foreseen, or to some extent even realized very rapidly, once the war had started. The naval arms race for more surface warships resulted in ever more valuable targets which needed more and more protection; yet the ships built were not to be of critical import to the outcome of the subsequent war. Devoting the resources to submarines and torpedoes could have crucially affected the outcome. Developing anti-submarine warfare techniques in anticipation of the threat of war could have paid great dividends. There was insufficient time for aircraft to be developed for more effective maritime use, given the limitations in range, communications, navigation equipment and weapons at that time.

The inter-war period was a pause, although the lessons learned in the recent major conflict could have been better exploited in a time of rapid scientific advance. In general there was remarkably little progress, other than incremental improvements to weapon systems. It was a difficult time for resources for military equipment. Germany was constrained by the terms of the Versailles peace treaty, Russia was reeling under the post-Revolution chaos, and the US and Europe were increasingly inclined towards disarmament. Artificial constraints on naval ship tonnage negotiated at the 1921 Washington Naval Conference ensured that money for naval modernization remained scarce.

The new key element in any future naval conflict would be air power. In the United States, General Billy Mitchell tried to convince the many doubters of the future importance of aircraft in maritime battles, and was eventually court-martialled for his pains. His flamboyant demonstrations of attacks on surface vessels showed just how vulnerable ships had become to aerial bombardment. While fellow airmen shared his views on the potential, his naval colleagues were not convinced.[1] It would be 1940 before the potency of naval air power was fully realized with the sinking of the *Konigsberg*. The following year saw land-based air power sinking the *Prince of Wales* and the

Repulse. It was left to the Japanese to develop the aircraft-carrier as a powerful offensive weapon platform, which they used successfully against the Chinese before World War II. Other nations put aircraft on to ships more for defensive purposes, or with the intention of ferrying them between theatres of operations. The carrier grew in significance rapidly from 1941. At Pearl Harbor, the Japanese destroyed 311 US aircraft, sank two battleships, and caused major damage to a further three for the loss of a total of twenty-nine of their own aircraft. The lesson was well taken, and the US moved rapidly towards a carrier-based strategy. By the middle of 1942, the US carrier forces were able to defeat the numerically larger Japanese forces at Midway. The crucial factor was the attaining of air superiority, and part of this came through the benefits of new reconnaissance capabilities which technology was providing.[5]

For hundreds of years naval engagements had depended on visual sighting of enemy vessels. In modern times, reconnaissance by boats, balloons or aircraft, and the gathering of intelligence information, could help to find the enemy; but for a successful attack, visual target acquisition remained necessary. While warships were large vessels and could be seen at line of sight ranges in good weather, they disappeared in poor visibility, in fog and at night. Submarines had to be spotted while they were on the surface, which would normally be under cover of darkness. An alternative, though somewhat alarming, method of submarine spotting was to back project the tell-tale line of bubbles from a launched torpedo. For observing the surface of the oceans, the development of radar from 1938 onwards dramatically changed the picture. Radar could make ships or submarines on the surface visible out to the line of sight horizon by day or night, and virtually regardless of the weather. Mounting radar in aircraft from 1941 onwards extended the radar horizon, so that ships and submarines could no longer depend on the cover of darkness to move or to surface. Ships' radars reduced the risk of surprise by the enemy from the air or from the sea. The Americans' technological advantage in having warning of the enemy through radar was a significant contribution to success at Midway. In many respects the maritime environment is ideal for radar use. Ships have high radar contrast against the uniform background of the sea. They also move relatively slowly and considerable information can be built up from comparatively few airborne radar sensors.

Radar could only help in the anti-submarine battle when the submarine was on the surface. The sea is opaque to electromagnetic radiation at radar frequencies. For detection beneath the sea, the passive hydrophone, which listened for the noise of passing submarines, was supplemented by a system analogous to radar: ASDIC.[6] The use of reflected sound pulses to detect underwater targets had been under development since the end of World War I. Indeed the progress achieved gave the British undue confidence in their ability to detect and destroy enemy submarines in any future conflict. Compared with radar in air, acoustic energy in water travels less predictable distances, suffers propagation anomalies and is not very discriminating. Nevertheless, the development of techniques for locating submerged submarines was a vital step forward in maritime warfare.

Both radar and ASDIC brought with them new vulnerabilities. Emitting a pulse of sound or radar energy gives information to the enemy. The outgoing pulse is necessarily much more intense than any reflected echo. The target will thus know that it is being subjected to attention at greater ranges than the return pulses can be detected by the sensor operator. Using passive detection systems, the hunted can become the hunter, and the surveillance system can become a homing beacon for the attacker. As we shall see later, new capabilities are often limited by the vulnerabilities that they carry with them.

The experiences of World War II signalled the end of the battleship as the centrepiece of sea power. It would continue to have a role in coastal bombardment and in projecting naval presence, but the flexibility and offensive range of air-delivered systems meant that its traditional role would be taken over by the aircraft-carrier. The technical developments which were coming to fruition at the end of the war were to have profound effects on maritime operations. Atomic research had produced both nuclear weapons and nuclear power sources. Air-breathing missiles and ballistic rockets had been used as weapon delivery systems. The jet aircraft had entered service. In World War II these innovations had been directed towards land and air operations; after the war, they were absorbed into naval operations with dramatic effect.

For propulsion, steam power changed the nature of naval warfare in the last century. It carried with it a penalty in the form of the need for logistic support. Nuclear power offers the prospect of virtually limitless range and motive power, without the need for continual resupply of fuel. It could make navies independent of either overseas bases or their armadas of support vessels. In the days before global satellite reconnaissance, a nuclear power plant could allow ships the freedom to roam over the oceans and keep their location and intentions secret. As with so many technical advances, nuclear power also brought some penalties. The reactor, associated power conversion system and shielding are bulky, heavy and expensive. Indeed the cost/size penalty is so great that it has only proved practical to use nuclear power plants for the largest surface ships. Even for these modern Dreadnoughts, it can be argued that the advantages are not great. In modern naval warfare, surface ships do not operate independently. They have a flotilla of defensive ships, all of which in turn require support, and the freedom of action is therefore already constrained. In 1988, there were only sixteen nuclear-powered warships in the world (five US aircraft carriers, nine US and two Soviet guided-missile cruisers).[7] Technology was able to provide the answer to the sailor's dream of limitless power to give speed and range, and yet be independent of base support; but at a price which made it impracticable.

Part of the lack of attraction for nuclear propulsion resulted from the development of an efficient alternative. The jet engine had been developed in the context of a better power plant for aircraft to enable them to operate at higher speeds. The high power, and good power to weight ratios, of the engine made it attractive to naval engineers. Easier to maintain and requiring less manpower, jet engines have subsequently become the general replacement for the petrol, diesel and coal plants of the past.

There was one aspect of sea power in which the advantages of nuclear power plants outweighed the cost and weight penalties. Submarines, when submerged, must operate with a power source which does not need oxygen in order to burn its fuel. It is easy to forget that the air is an essential part of the fuel of all the vehicles, boats and aircraft that operate around us. Oil-based fuels need oxygen to burn and produce power in an engine. Air is a commodity in short supply in a submerged submarine. Electric motors provided a ready answer to the problem, but had limitations. They needed batteries as their energy source, and the batteries needed regular recharging. To do this the submarine would have to come near the surface, and run its diesel engine as a battery charger. Taking in air and exhausting burnt fuel, the submarine was vulnerable to detection and to attack, while at the same time lacking the variety of defensive armament available to surface vessels. Nuclear power can provide virtually unlimited motive power without the need to surface, and can also recirculate the air for the crew to breathe, and purify the sea water for drinking. The power allows the submarine to operate at high speed if necessary, and stay submerged as long as the crew's rations last. By transforming the survivability of the submarine, the nuclear power plant becomes a technological innovation worth paying for. There are currently 375 nuclear-powered submarines operating around the world in five navies.[8]

In the author's view, the nuclear-powered submarine has assumed the mantle of the flagship of sea power: a title held only briefly by the aircraft-carrier after it took it from the battleship. The nuclear power plant has caused the submarine to grow in size—the Soviet Typhoon

class displaces 25,000 tons[9]—and in firepower. It is undetectable
except when coming in for an attack, and has freedom to roam the
oceans worldwide. There are those who would argue that it cannot
replace the major surface warship, on the grounds that its invisibility
means that it cannot project power. This view carries less weight in
the light of the experiences of the Falklands conflict of 1982. The
possibility of a nuclear-powered submarine being in the area of the
Falklands ahead of the Task Force allowed the British government
to declare an exclusion zone at an early stage. The sinking of the
Argentinian warship, *General Belgrano*, by a nuclear-powered submarine caused the Argentinian navy to seek safe refuge in mainland ports,
and hence gave the British control of the sea. Notwithstanding this
control, the Royal Navy had to expend considerable effort in guarding
against the possibility of a submarine attack by one of Argentina's
three submarines. The evidence of the critical importance of the submarine in two world wars has been confirmed in the 1980s by the
Falklands conflict. Submarines were already powerful but the advent
of nuclear power has given them flexibility and invulnerability. However, as yet the submarine lacks the ability to control the airspace
above the ocean.

While technology has provided the power source which could allow
submarines to operate with true freedom, the weapon systems of both
surface and sub-surface vessels have also been completely transformed in the post-war era. Ship main armament had not increased
in calibre, range or firepower significantly since the days of the Dreadnoughts. Improvements had come from measures to improve accuracy and control. The development of missile technology offered
major increases in range of offensive weaponry, with further
improvements in accuracy and the capability of increased destructive
power. Each missile costs far more than a shell for a naval gun, but a
ship armed only with guns must always be at risk to an adversary able
to fire missiles at distances beyond gun range. The advent of the
missile has therefore relegated the gun to the role of shore bombardment, close attack against a poorly defended enemy vessel, and terminal air defence using modern rapid fire systems.

For attacking other ships, cruise missiles have taken over the role
of the guns. The biggest guns (the US 16″ calibre) have a maximum
range of 40km over which distance they have an accuracy of around
550 metres, and can fire only two rounds per minute.[10] A Tomahawk
cruise missile can carry 1,000lbs of high explosive a distance of 460km
and with its terminal radar guidance will hit the target. The land
attack version operates out to 1,300km with an accuracy of better
than ten metres.[11] The range, explosive power and accuracy of these
modern missile systems has changed the nature of naval warfare yet

again. Given intelligence through airborne or satellite reconnaissance, or from other sources, a ship can be attacked from over the horizon. As always this progress carries with it a penalty. Each Tomahawk missile cost $1.27m. in 1982. The shorter ranged (110km/500lbs HE) Harpoon missile was estimated to cost $940,000 per round.[12] Against these enormous costs must be set the effectiveness of the weapons. In 1967, the Israeli destroyer, *Eilat*, was sunk by Egyptian Styx missiles fired from coastal patrol boats. In 1982, the Royal Navy destroyer HMS *Sheffield* was sunk by an air-launched version of the Exocet cruise missile. An Exocet costs about $250,000,[13] which is about one thousandth the cost of a modern destroyer. The power of the missile makes it a key factor in modern naval warfare. While it is expensive, its targets are enormously more costly. The threat to surface ships can come from missiles launched from other ships, from aircraft, from land-based systems or from submarine launched missiles.

Each new threat spawns research into countermeasures. Here again the missile has assumed a major role. To defend itself, a ship can attempt to destroy the missile launch platform. Surface-to-air missiles engage attacking aircraft, surface-to-surface missiles attempt to beat potential attackers to the draw, anti-submarine rocket-delivered depth charges and torpedoes defend against submarines. To prevent incoming missiles reaching their targets various defensive measures are taken. Some missiles use radar-homing, and the target ship can use electronic counter-measures to deceive the missile sensors. When infra-red homing is used, decoy hot sources may be employed to deflect the incoming weapon. Cruise missiles travel at similar speeds to aircraft, and missile and gun defences can also be used against them.

Nuclear-powered submarines, missiles, radar, air power and maritime surveillance systems have all changed the face of naval warfare. Yet there is one development which has complicated predictions of future maritime operations more than all the rest put together. In the immediate postwar period, atomic weapons were so expensive, so difficult to construct, so large and so critical to strategic plans that they seemed to have limited relevance to future sea battles. With the development of tactical nuclear weapons of small physical size and limited explosive yield, it became possible to give virtually every naval weapon a nuclear capability. A depth charge which uses a nuclear explosion offers a much greater prospect of destroying or disabling a submarine once its position has been roughly located. A nuclear warhead can be fitted to a torpedo. A nuclear missile launched from an aircraft, a land base, a surface ship or a submarine can destroy any ship once it has been located, identified and is within range. That range will be several hundred miles. Nuclear weapons thus give naval firepower a very high probability of success in destroying their targets while at the same time giving naval weapon platforms much greater vulnerability when facing a nuclear armed enemy.

Opinions vary as to the utility of such naval nuclear warfighting systems. The special constraints afforded to nuclear weapons, in the light of the dangers of escalation to strategic nuclear exchange, could operate in two differing ways. It could be argued that a maritime engagement allowed the use of nuclear weapons with no risk of collateral damage, and with relatively easy escalation control. In some future conflict, the political judgement could be that resolve could be signalled by the use of a nuclear torpedo. The other view would be that the release of nuclear weapons would be such a critical decision, and such a change in the nature of the conflict, that it would be unlikely to be made for a naval engagement, the outcome of which would not directly affect the overall advance of the enemy.

The most dramatic effect of nuclear weapons on naval operations has been the emergence of a new role of overwhelming importance. The bringing together of the nuclear-powered submarine and the long-range nuclear warhead missile has brought a new element to warfare. Nuclear weapons have not been used in anger since World War II; the fear of nuclear retaliation has deterred nations from employing them. A key element in this strategy of nuclear deterrence is the requirement for a military capability to inflict an unacceptable level of damage in retaliation on an enemy, regardless of any pre-emptive action the enemy might take. Nuclear-powered submarines can remain hidden under the sea for months. Armed with ballistic missiles carrying multiple nuclear warheads, they can threaten retribution from anywhere in vast areas of the oceans. Undetectable, and hence invulnerable, they are the most credible part of a nuclear nation's nuclear forces. In addition, as the accuracy of such weapon systems increase, there is considerable advantage in replacing land-based nuclear systems with appropriately equipped submarines.

This rapid review of the major technical developments which have changed the nature of maritime warfare over the past two centuries has taken as read the need for sea power. Before the nuclear age, the importance of control of the sea was easily understood. Sea-going nations had provided navies for a number of purposes: to protect their trade routes; to secure overseas possessions; to deter other nations from war; and to secure their sea lines of communication in war. In the early years of the nuclear age, when nuclear bombs were scarce and air-delivered, the major naval powers could expect their roles in the next war to be little changed from the last. Once nuclear weapons became plentiful, delivery systems accurate and varied, surveillance systems global and thermo-nuclear war scenarios notable for their brevity, the roles of navies became more difficult to predict.

If nuclear weapons were used extensively in a future war, and ports and harbours were included as targets, it could be argued that the protection of merchant shipping becomes an irrelevance. Sea power is exercised in slow time, and strategists suggested that a nuclear war, once started, looked like being over on the land before the further supplies, troops and equipment brought by sea could influence the outcome. However, the very power of nuclear weapons has made their use in war less than certain. In a world where NATO and the Warsaw Pact each has an assured capability to destroy the other in a general nuclear war, there remains a need to be prepared for non-nuclear conflict. An ability to fight a conventional war makes it more believable that a nation, or an alliance, would be prepared to defend itself. In NATO's case, troops and equipment must travel from North America and the United Kingdom to reinforce Europe if war becomes likely. Protection of the sea lines of communication thus becomes a vital task to demonstrate the capability to fight a conventional war against the Warsaw Pact. If deterrence failed and such a war started, both sides would have considerable incentives to prevent it developing into an all-out nuclear exchange. Securing the sea lanes would reduce the pressure on NATO to use nuclear weapons at an early stage, if the reinforcements allowed it to maintain its fighting capability at the non-nuclear level. In a superpower conflict conventional naval power has a role.

The experience of the past forty years suggests that while world war can be deterred, lower level conflict continues unabated. Traditionally naval power has had an important role in deterring such conflict ('showing the flag') and in dealing with it. Here there are indications that technology is changing the nature of such operations. The power of modern missile systems can mean that a militarily inferior state can threaten a major naval power. Protecting trade routes becomes more difficult, both because of the diversity of threats and also because of the nature of the modern international system. Western nations are concerned about the security of their oil supply routes, and this has called for international mine-clearing operations in the Gulf. When merchant shipping is put at risk by third parties engaged in war, naval power is needed to protect them. As has been seen in the Iran-Iraq war in 1988, this protection may extend to the use of offensive naval operations to protect the passage of tankers. The Falklands conflict of 1982 gave an example of the modern use of sea power to secure a nation's overseas possessions. Those nations with such commitments will need the balanced military forces necessary for such operations. However, as effective counter-measures become available to third world nations through new weapon systems, the retention of the large scale capability to intervene by sea will become increasingly expensive.

Looking for the lessons to be learned from the major technical changes to maritime capability, it is possible to draw out certain common factors. These are combat performance areas where a qualitative change results in a significant enhancement (or limitation) in naval power. The recurring areas, which are not mutually exclusive, are: speed and manoeuvrability; firepower and accuracy; radius of action; detection and detectability; vulnerability and survivability; support requirements; and, finally, cost-effectiveness. In examining the application of current technical advances to future maritime operations, it will be worth looking at the probable implications for these areas first. It may be that other factors, such as arms control, political constraints, manpower, training, communications, or fuel availability, become additional considerations. We examine these questions in the last part of this book.

The last point that can be extracted from the history of naval technology is the time that has elapsed between the critical scientific advance and the widespread deployment of the resulting weapon systems. It took around forty years between the building of the first steamboat, the first submarine and the flight of the first aircraft, and the subsequent deployment of effective forces of steam-powered warships, U-boats and aircraft-carriers respectively. For guided-weapon destroyers and nuclear submarines the timescale was nearer twenty years. There are no indications that the gestation period is shortening. Indeed, since the advent of the nuclear submarine developments have been incremental in capability rather than revolutionary. While hovercraft, helicopters, and hydrofoils have produced novel opportunities, they have not changed the nature of maritime warfare in the sense of the previous examples. An examination of the current areas of research will indicate which offer the greatest benefits in future naval warfare.

CHAPTER 3

Land Warfare

IN THE nuclear age it is all too easy to dismiss land warfare as of decreasing importance. High technology seems to offer more and more for the world's navies and air forces, while armies remain equipped with weapons little different from those used in World War II. Yet armies still make up the major element of nations' military might, and there are more than eighteen million full-time soldiers in the world's ground forces. Significant changes in army methods of operation have followed technical developments in the past and an examination of these will indicate the most likely areas for future innovation.

In early days land warfare was comparatively small scale. One estimate of the total killed in war in France, England, Austria-Hungary and Russia between 1101 and 1599 comes to just over one million men. The comparative figure for the seventeenth century alone was 2.5 million, rising to 3.6 million for the next century.[1] Weapon development was directed towards increasing the range of action of weapons, increasing their effectiveness and increasing the rate of weapon delivery. The longbow gave the English at Crécy in 1346 a crucial advantage over the French forces. Yet the bow was not a novel technical breakthrough: its successes in the past had been largely ignored. Indeed it is surprising how often the weapons which alter the whole conduct of land warfare are not the technological novelties, but the thoughtful application of well-understood techniques. Gunpowder gave hand-guns, cannons and rockets increased range and firepower from the fourteenth century onwards. Experience in combat, progress in chemistry, mathematics and engineering, all improved armies' killing power. As with maritime warfare, the more significant technological advances date from the beginning of the last century.

By the early 1800s infantry were equipped with inaccurate and expensive muskets, which took a considerable time to reload. Advances in chemistry at the turn of the century had produced fulminates of silver and mercury: explosives which detonated when struck. Their use for igniting the powder in the gun barrel much reduced

19

the incidence of misfires in flintlocks. Once the cylindroconoidal bullet had been designed in 1823, it could be coupled to the percussion cap to make the rifle bullet,[2] A gun that fired a bullet which sealed itself into the bore, which was rifled, offered greater range and accuracy with quicker loading. Improvements in manufacturing technology allowed breechloading to become practical and dramatically increase the rate of fire. The industrial revolution was also changing the way in which such guns could be produced. Instead of the hand-crafted individual weapon, the mass production of standard parts became the norm. The cost of weapons could decrease as their effectiveness was increasing. The American Civil War demonstrated the power of these new infantry weapons. The repeating rifle improved rates of fire yet further, but brought with it the penalty of much greater ammunition requirements. Already it was becoming apparent that the vulnerability of the horse and rider to long-range rifle fire had made the cavalry decreasingly effective as a means of shock action.

The repeating rifle offered the prospect of yet more concentrated fire if the reloading requirement could be reduced, and if the rate of fire could be increased. During the second half of the nineteenth century work was done on both these aspects. The French produced a 37-barrel gun, which weighed one ton, and could deliver its load of ten shells per barrel in one minute.[3] Richard Gatling produced the first machine-gun in 1862. This multi-barrelled weapon used a purely mechanical action to load, fire and eject spent cartridges. The energy to activate the mechanism was provided by a hand crank. Hiram Maxim contributed to the further development of the machine-gun by adapting it so that the recoil energy from each shot was used to operate the mechanism. This was the first automatic machine-gun. The century had seen rates of fire improve a thousandfold.

The innovations in the design and the development of infantry weapons were also incorporated in artillery guns. Rifling of barrels and breech-loading improved accuracy, range and rate of fire from the middle of the century onwards. Science was providing a greater understanding of the physics of the guns, and better materials and manufacturing processes. The strength of the barrels was improved while the overall weight could be relatively less. Guns became more powerful and more mobile. It was late in the century before satisfactory recoil mechanisms were adopted, which allowed the gun to absorb the reaction to the firing of the shell and return to the firing position. Such mechanisms allowed increased rates of fire. Mathematical work on ballistics theory improved accuracy. Although Shrapnel had filled a hollow shell with shot in 1784, it was nearly another seventy years before a reliable fuse was perfected.[4] One further development improved artillery effectiveness: the invention of smokeless powders. The lack of smoke from propellants such as cordite aided concealment of gun positions and reduced obscuration of targets. More importantly, the new powders were slow burning. This meant that pressures rose progressively and barrels could be longer and bores be larger. Range, accuracy and firepower all benefited. The new opportunity to fill the projectile with a high explosive charge further increased the destructive power.

Guns could fire shells weighing 12lbs each at a rate of twenty shells per minute. There were large numbers of guns available as manufacturing processes became more standardized. The ammunition requirement for any campaign became a crucial factor in planning. One apparently non-military invention was to have dramatic strategic significance in the moving of men and matériel for war. The Stockton to Darlington railway opened in 1825, and the railroad spread with a speed characteristic of commercial rather than military progress. The military were slower to realize the contribution that the railroad could make to their deployment and logistic support plans. The strategic use of railways in the American Civil War (1861–65) and the Austro-Prussian War of 1866 showed that great advantage could be gained by the imaginative use of these fast supply lines, which can carry large quantities of cargo. In 1870 von Moltke, the Prussian Chief of the General Staff, mobilized and moved three armies, totalling 384,000 men, to face the French west of the Rhine in just eighteen days. With the railroad it became possible to envisage supporting massive operations at considerable distances. At the same time, armies could become dependent on these fixed and known lines, and hence were vulnerable to counter-measures taken against the railroads.

The telegraph paralleled the railroad in its development both chronologically and geographically. Once Samuel Morse had convinced the doubters of its merits, commercial interests ensured that the telegraph spread rapidly, particularly in expanding North America. The military advantages of instant communication are enormous. When communication is at the speed of the horse and messenger, plans must be rigid and rapid reaction to changing circumstances becomes impractical. With the aid of the telegraph, strategic information about the actions of the enemy could be passed in time for preventive action to be taken. Public information about the course of battles became available from war correspondents. Commanders could apply reserve forces at all levels in a much more effective way. Large forces could be controlled. Artillery fire could be directed on to targets by direct communication between spotter and battery. The telegraph and telephone (1876) quickened the pace of warfare by shortening response times and increasing flexibility. Coupling this speed of information communication with the effect of the railroad

TT—C

on speed of movement, the nature of land warfare is changed in scale by two primarily civil inventions.

Just as steam power, diesel engines and eventually nuclear plants transformed the nature of naval warfare, the move from animal power to mechanical drives revolutionized land operations. Steam power influenced strategy because the size of the engines restricted employment on land to the railways. Logistic support plans had therefore to follow the routes of the railway lines. Work in the mid-nineteenth century led to Nikolaus August Otto developing a four-stroke internal combustion engine by 1876. The early engine-driven Benz four-wheel automobiles were marketed from 1890 onwards. The motor car was a commercial proposition. Yet the application of this technology to warfare seems inexplicably slow in retrospect. All the components for the tank had been invented by the turn of the century, and the basic concept was centuries old, but it would be the middle of World War I before they would be assembled and fielded in battle. Artillery would continue to be dragged into position by horse, and men would march unprotected to their fighting posts.

The credit for the eventual production of the tank goes to the persistence of Colonel Ernest Swinton of the British Army.[5] Despite War Office antipathy, but with the support of Winston Churchill (and the Admiralty), work progressed from 1914 onwards. The use of tanks at the battle of Cambrai in 1917 was every bit as significant in the history of land warfare as the longbow had been at Crécy. The stagnated trench warfare could be ended by the new weapon system. Armoured vehicles with caterpillar tracks for cross-country capability and integral firepower could provide offensive action that would break through heavily-defended positions. Even these lessons were not absorbed quickly and the full potential of the tank was not exploited during the war. The 540 tanks of the British used at Amiens on 8 August 1918 made it a significant victory, and brought an end to the stand-off debilitating warfare of the past four years.[6]

What was it that made World War I the succession of stagnated defensive battles? The machine-gun had been adopted widely by all combatants and could be produced in large numbers. The industrialization of society allowed armament to be produced in continuous and unprecedented quantities. The railways endlessly delivered men and ammunition into the war. Equally important, the low technology of preparing defensive positions had a critical influence on the nature of the warfare. Barbed wire had been patented in America in 1867, and the copious quantities needed to tame the West led to cheap manufacturing processes. The low cost, ease of emplacement and effectiveness in slowing infantry movement of barbed wire defences allowed the machine-gun to prevent forward movement. With no counter to these prepared defensive positions, and the massive use of artillery leading to the universal use of trenches, offensive action inevitably brought casualty figures never previously contemplated. Mass production had led to mass destruction.

One technological approach to overcome the impenetrability of the defence was the use of disabling chemical agents. Despite the international prohibition on the use of poison gases in The Hague Convention, the first gas attack was made against the Allied forces at Ypres on 22 April 1915. Five thousand casualties and the loss of sixty field guns was the result.[7] The use by both sides of chemical killing and incapacitating munitions escalated rapidly.[8] What was a novel technological breakthrough did not lead to a strategic advantage. The counter-measures of gas masks and protection reduced what was already an imprecise weapon to a level of effectiveness somewhat less than that of conventional artillery. Nevertheless, the unseen killer gas did have profoundly greater demoralizing effects on troops under attack than the more obvious—and lethal—high explosive shells.

Technology had provided one extra element to the land battle in the run-up to the World War I: the aeroplane. How that affected warfare is considered in the next Chapter; but in the context of the land battles of World War I, it was another potential war-winning element which suffered from lack of exploitation. Inventions which had enjoyed success and development from civilian manufacturers for commercial reasons were not adopted with sufficient imagination to change tactics. Where science was applied, it was to increase the destructive power of artillery, the rate of fire of infantry and the killing power of munitions. The need to harness and exploit already-developed civilian novelties such as the motor car, the tractor and the aircraft was only slowly appreciated. Yet these devices held the key to new battlefield tactics which could have broken the stalemate of trench warfare.

If limited use of tanks had indicated a way to escape trench warfare, it was scarcely surprising that the next two decades saw much thought devoted to the role and improvement of the armoured fighting vehicle. It is interesting that there are a number of examples of such high priority development in the light of only slight combat experience. These include the pre-World War I battleships, the strategic bomber after the 1917 air raids on London and nuclear weaponry after the 1945 attacks on Hiroshima and Nagasaki. The inter-war period saw strong advocates of the importance of armour in future conflicts.[9] The Western establishment was orientated towards peace and disarmament, views which did not sit well with the development of so overtly offensive a weapon as the tank. Emphasis was given to defensive measures and the use of the tank in support of the infantry.

In Germany the climate of opinion was markedly different. Looking for a means of achieving a rapid breakthrough capability, the use of tanks, artillery and motorized infantry was seen as of first importance. The new tactical concept of operations, subsequently known as *Blitzkrieg*, sought to achieve rapid breakthrough using armour supported by artillery and air power. Tanks developed through improvements in engines, guns, gyroscopic stabilization of weapons and armour.

What research was there into measures to counter the power of the tank? Field artillery had been used in this role in World War I, and specialist guns were developed with sufficient power to penetrate armour in the inter-war period. It was to be 1942 before the infantry began to gain an effective anti-tank capability with rocket-propelled launchers. Land mines were made more effective, but still required laborious preparation and remained a defensive rather than offensive weapon.

Indeed it was improvements in defensive measures which engendered most interest amongst the Allies. The Maginot Line of defensive fortifications in Europe used massive engineering works to provide an impenetrable defensive network against an enemy using World War I tactics. Technology could provide such a barrier, but when the enemy used unexpected tactics the magnificent static system of defence had little relevance.

So what was technology offering the land forces for World War II, and how did the promises match performance under combat conditions? Motorized transport had become universal in the inter-war period, and thus men and stores were less constrained to the straight lines of the railways. Communications had made great advances. While wireless telegraphy was widely available in the previous war, the full exploitation of radio had to await the development of radio transmission and reception techniques based on thermionic valves. The triode valve had been invented in 1906 and modulation of radio frequency carrier waves by audio signals demonstrated. The British army formed its first wireless company in 1911; but the transmitter/receiver weighed two tons and was horse-drawn. The rapid development of radio-telephone owed more to the commercial pressures of broadcasting than military research in the immediate postwar era. Mass markets for radio receivers brought down costs as performance improved. Amateur and professional users explored the propagation characteristics of different frequencies under changing ionospheric conditions. By 1939 the radio receiver was a familiar household piece of apparatus, and the developments in thermionic valves had allowed both powerful transmitters and sensitive receivers to be mass produced. For the army portable radio equipment was standard.

The ability for higher formation to communicate with lower and

for commanders to talk directly to their troops, and all at the speed
of light, was the key to capitalizing on the new mobility and flexibility
of motorized forces. This was an area of development which was
recognized to be important. Commercial exploitation of radio (and in
time television) led to reduced production costs and improved
reliability. Realizing the advantages of radio communications to land
forces, it would have been productive to devote equal effort to
methods of denying such communications to an enemy. Nevertheless,
considerable success was achieved through interception of radio mes-
sages as an intelligence-gathering method. Technology had provided
a new capability to control forces in short timescales, but was also to
make armies dependent on a medium which could be intercepted,
located and eventually disrupted.

In the area of munitions, inter-war development was mainly
incremental. Manufacturing techniques were improved and, coupled
with better designs, improvements in accuracy and reliability were
achieved. While radar was of great significance to both the sea and
the air battles of World War II, the problem of clutter from ground
reflections of radar waves meant that it was not used for the detection
of enemy land forces. One important use for radar over land was
found. In 1942, the first tests were conducted of shells containing
their own radar by which they could accurately measure their height
above the ground. The altitude measurement was used to explode
the shell at pre-set low height above the ground to give maximum
fragmentation effect. Shrapnel's work of the eighteenth century was
coming to fruition. Such proximity-fused shells proved extremely
effective against German troops from the end of 1944 onwards.

The artillery itself had not increased in calibre but new fire control
systems improved accuracy and reliability. Motor transport ensured
rapid resupply of ammunition, and gave mobility to artillery batteries.
Fire control and radio gave much greater scope for accurate co-ordinated barrages using dispersed batteries against a common target.
The Russians brought back the long-out-of-favour rocket as a major
contribution to artillery firepower. Trucks carried twelve or sixteen
rocket-launchers which could be used to fire a salvo.

The tank had spawned special purpose variants to clear minefields
and provide engineering support and some with light armour to
improve speed and manoeuvrability. Infantry could be transported
in armoured vehicles. Surprisingly, the development of the tank in
the inter-war period had not generated a range of effective anti-tank
weapons, apart from the tank itself. Indeed, development of counters
to tanks in general was an area in which research could have paid
great dividends. Work on the shaped charge, with its high penetration
ability against armoured plate, and the use of high velocity guns and

the development of the bazooka during the war redressed the lack of earlier work to some extent. However, in the early days of the war the combination of tanks and aircraft in fast-moving co-ordinated offensive thrusts proved to be highly successful in achieving rapid advances. Technology had provided the wherewithal for the new tactical doctrine of *Blitzkrieg*, and the defensive palliatives of the last war were inadequate to meet the new challenge.[10]

This is not to say that technology had not been able to provide improvements to defensive equipment. Mass production techniques had made large quantities of land mines available. Minefields could be laid rapidly, and were increasingly difficult to clear. They were used to slow enemy advance or, in the case of forces such as the Russians who chose to ignore such obstacles, to inflict considerable casualties. Significant advances were also made in the field of camouflage and smoke-screen generation, which gave forces higher survivability and the possibility of greater tactical surprise.

In the transporting of land forces, the use of aircraft allowed new concepts of operations to be explored through the use of airborne forces. We shall consider this further in the next Chapter. Specialist vehicles for amphibious operations were also developed. The legendary DUKW, a cross between a lorry and a boat, was not a great technological breakthrough as an amphibious troop-carrier. Like the tank in the previous war, it was the bringing together of mature technologies in an innovative way. Again, it was necessary to convince a sceptical military establishment of the military effectiveness of such an obvious and simple idea. In many cases the application of already mature technologies is a characteristic of the more successful army equipment improvements. This may be a reflection of the large quantities of equipment necessary for any army re-equipment programme, and hence the attractions of lower unit costs, through the use of technologies already proven in the civil sector.

While the nature of warfare had changed dramatically between the two world wars, ground forces still found themselves in attrition battles. Despite the strategic, technological and economic advantages which the US forces enjoyed over Japan by 1945, they expected losses numbering hundreds of thousands in the final operations to bring about its defeat. In the event, the Japanese surrender was brought about by the strategic use of atomic weapons at Hiroshima and Nagasaki in August 1945. This winning of the land battle by the use of atomic air power led many to discount the future importance of non-nuclear land forces.

The early atomic weapons were large, heavy, expensive and scarce. Their delivery by air drop against major economic targets appeared greatly to diminish the relevance of the land battle. Two developments were to change this premature assessment. First, all conflicts since 1945 have been non-nuclear, and some have required very large ground force involvement. Secondly, nuclear weapons were not to remain the rare, bulky and impossibly expensive munitions that they were at first. The advent of thermonuclear weapons from 1952 onwards led not only to the possibility of ever more powerful strategic weapons, but also to much smaller tactical nuclear warheads. Coupled with progress in missile technology, armies could be equipped with short-range nuclear armed rockets for use against purely military targets. Nuclear weapons became cheaper and easier to build, and initially the prospect of such devastating firepower appeared inviting to the armies of the nuclear states. The threat of a nuclear attack changed the traditional military virtue of concentration of force into a new vulnerability. If armies were to be able to survive a nuclear attack, they must disperse. Thus the possession of army tactical nuclear systems could force a potential enemy into deploying in a disadvantageous way without a shot being fired. As nuclear miniaturization proceeded, nuclear warheads were fitted in artillery shells. The potential firepower effect of an artillery barrage was increased by many orders of magnitude.

Science had given armies explosive power beyond all previous experience. It posed the nuclear armies with considerable problems in preparing for future wars. If nuclear missiles, mines, and artillery were available to both sides and were to be used on the battlefield, losses would be enormous in very short timescales. It was difficult to visualize armies being able to make cohesive progress in the aftermath of an exchange of battlefield nuclear weapons. In addition, the strategic implications of the use of these tactical weapons could not be forgotten. The high risk of escalation from battlefield nuclear weapons being used against military targets to strategic nuclear weapons being used against population centres, meant that even the lowest-yielding tactical nuclear weapon would remain under firm political control. While science could provide weapons of great power for the army, the consequences of their use are so great that they become virtually unusable. This does not discount the role they play in deterrence, in that they provide a possible link from conventional conflict to a strategic nuclear exchange. In the conflicts which have been fought since 1945 around the world, they have played no part.

If the advent of the nuclear weapon has had less effect on armies than was originally anticipated, how have land forces used nuclear power technology? We saw in the previous Chapter that nuclear power was an expensive option for navies, and its advantages only outweighed its cost in the case of the submarine. Heavy, expensive and requiring highly technical support, nuclear power plants have found no army vehicle to propel as yet. Indeed, power sources have changed little from the internal combustion engines developed at the start of the century. The gas turbine has been incorporated into some tank drives, but as yet offers no overriding advantages.

Tanks have been developed in the postwar period to move at higher speeds, carry greater firepower, have more mobility and improved armour protection. These aspects of tank design are interdependent, and many modern changes in design reflect differing judgements on relative priorities as much as technological breakthroughs. New materials can offer improved protection without the consequent increase in weight of additional armour plate. Tank main armament has also improved in flexibility, rate of fire and accuracy both through gun design and fire control system development. Nevertheless, just as the motor car today operates in much the same way as the car of the 1920s, so the tank seems to have long passed the peak in innovative design. At the end of World War I it was a totally new concept which could break the deadlock of trench warfare. At the start of World War II, the tank could make rapid advances possible through the use of imaginative tactics. By the end of that war, it had become a normal part of an army's inventory, and was no longer the decisive weapon. Little has happened to the design of tanks in the last forty years to make them once again the battle-winning weapon system.

Important research in this postwar period has been into ways of countering the tank. A tank can be destroyed by mines, missiles or guns. The mines can be laid by the ground forces, fired by artillery or dropped from the air. Missiles can be fired from the ground, launched from aircraft or operated from hand-held infantry systems. The guns can be high velocity mounted on other tanks, specialist air or surface systems, or hand-held recoilless rifles. The proliferation of anti-tank munitions of increasing power over a period of forty years, which at the same time has given remarkably little battle experience of mass tank warfare, makes the contribution of the tank in future wars arguable. The advent of the armed helicopter, both as a tank killer and a tank replacement, is considered in the next Chapter, as are the implications of the helicopter for land force mobility.

Infantry transport has been developed to provide fast armoured personnel carriers, yet response times for forces have changed little. Armies need to transport enormous quantities of men and matériel, the bulk of which must travel on the earth's surface at speeds which reached their maximum half a century ago. However, the infantry-man has gained many new capabilities over this time. His personal weapon has improved in rate of fire, portability and accuracy. He can carry his communication system with him; it is automatically encoded to prevent interception and can change frequency automatically to reduce the effectiveness of electronic counter-measures. Radar allows him to pinpoint enemy artillery and mortar positions and, to a limited extent, detect enemy ground movements. He can carry potent anti-tank and air defence weapons. Postwar technology, through reducing the size of the weapon systems, has made the individual soldier a powerful weapon operator. Just as the torpedo and the missile threaten the capital ship, so the low cost hand-held anti-tank weapon can threaten the expensive tank.

In artillery, with the exception of the nuclear shells discussed earlier, the advances have been incremental in nature. Fire control systems have benefited from the development of smaller and more powerful computers, so that accurate co-ordinated fire can be con-trolled from multiple artillery batteries. Inertial navigation systems have improved the accuracy of weapon-aiming and of fire correction. The development of ballistic and cruise missiles for nuclear weapons has led to systems of sufficiently high accuracy for them to be con-sidered as options for conventional artillery. The possibilities and the costs of these options will be examined in Chapter 14. Unguided rockets have reappeared as a useful addition to an army's firepower, when coupled to modern surveillance and targeting systems.

For munitions, high explosive remains the major component of weapon stocks. Shells are custom-built to give greater effectiveness against particular target sets. Chemical weapons were developed extensively for use in World War II, but neither side used them. The nerve agents available today are potentially very effective against an unprotected enemy, and technology has provided relatively simple operating systems for such weapons. Protective measures have also improved very significantly. With so little experience of chemical war-fare, prediciton about its impact on future conflicts is liable to be very speculative. The reluctance of nations to use such weapons in the past, for fear of retaliation or international criticism, may mean that they will continue to have little impact on warfare, provided both sides see it as in their interest to refraim from their use. It is of concern that their use appeared to be increasing in the Iran–Iraq war, with exten-sive civilian casualties reported in 1988.

In one respect, it is possible to be confident that technology has changed the nature of future major conflict. Since war began, land fighting had been predominantly a daytime activity. Traditionally, attacks are made at dawn, the fighting continues through the day, and forces regroup and resupply by night. Technology can now give the soldier (and, as importantly, the airman) the ability to see at night virtually as well as by day. Image intensifiers can now be produced which can be worn with little more encumbrance than spectacles. Night sights give a true night firing ability. The widespread use of night vision aids may be one of the most significant products of post-war technology for land forces. The implications of continuous fighting for manpower, ammunition consumption, logistic support and vulnerability of the supply system are profound. Yet again experience is limited.

Any analysis of what prospects technology holds for the land forces of tomorrow must make assumptions about the roles of such forces. In Central Europe, NATO requires land and air forces to convince the Warsaw Pact that no easy conventional victory is available to it. NATO forces must, therefore, be able to prevent a rapid advance of Soviet forces. But if deterrence in Europe is maintained, land forces will find themselves fighting in other places in the world. Armies are needed for forms of conflict ranging from protecting nationals and controlling internal disorder, through terrorism and guerrilla war, to small and medium scale international wars. The search must be for equipment and tactics to fit the land forces for the many roles which they may be called upon to undertake; and to do it at an affordable price.

The rates of fire of modern weapon systems, and the greater depth of land warfare puts a great strain on the logistic chain. From manufacture, through stockpiles, to delivery, there must be sufficient ammunition, food and other supplies. The increasing costs of weapons make the costs of stockpiles a crucial aspect of defence budgeting. Yet however good the weapons system, it is useless once the ammunition supplies are exhausted.

This brief review of technological development in land warfare does not give much cause for optimism for the future. While the historian's benefit of hindsight is a great help, it does not appear that armies in peace have been able to spot the technologies which would give them major advantages in war. There have also been marked institutional pressures against changing to new tactical concepts to exploit the potential of new technologies. The lessons have certain parallels with the naval warfare cases examined in the previous Chapter. In respect of those areas which produced qualitative changes in effectiveness. Early weapon developments were in rates of fire and greater range, hence changing the nature of the battle. Changes in power sources gave flexibility and range to operations: the railway and the internal combustion engine revolutionized logistic support. Mass production brought mass destruction. The telegraph, telephone and wireless gave instantaneous communication and control, changing the way land forces could be used. Major weapon systems have become more vulnerable to much cheaper portable weapons.

For the future, land forces will be required for all the roles which they have had in the past. They will need to enhance their capabilities in four areas. First, they will need timely and accurate intelligence both at the strategic and tactical level, if the forces are to be used effectively. Secondly, the forces will need mobility to deploy to theatres of operations and, once there, to fighting positions. Thirdly, the soldier's firepower must be developed to provide the right effect at the minimum cost. Finally, as the enemy develops his ability to fight the land war, the survivability of man and machine will be an increasing problem.

CHAPTER 4

Air and Space Warfare

WHILE it is possible to draw upon thousands of years of the history of warfare for both land and sea, most of the development of air warfare has taken place in this century. It is therefore much more difficult to take the historical perspective as to which technical developments have been of greatest significance, but there is no doubt that the aircraft itself has changed the whole nature of warfare.

The use of balloons as artillery observation posts was well tried by the end of the nineteenth century. They provided convenient 'high ground' where nature had omitted to fill the military need. Even more than the naval sail ships, they were at the mercy of the wind and were normally tethered. It was the technical development which allowed man to choose his path through the air which was crucial. The combination of a lighter-than-air vehicle with internal combustion engine and air propeller was the obvious route. Indeed the military followed this development line with some enthusiasm before World War I. The search for more power and greater range increased the engine and fuel weight, which in turn required ever larger displacements to support the weight. The potential of the airship was limited by the laws of physics from the outset. Nevertheless, their range and payload in the early days of air warfare did contribute to future strategic thinking. The raids by German Zeppelins in the early part of the war showed that air power could take the war right back to the opponent's homeland, which had previously been thought of as a safe refuge.

The longer-term development of air power was to be through the heavier-than-air route. Otto Lilienthal developed the glider in the last quarter of the nineteenth century and, from the experience of over 2,000 flights, was able to point the way towards the design of powered aircraft. In 1896 an unmanned steam-driven aircraft made a successful flight, and on 17 December 1903 the Wright brothers demonstrated the first heavier-than-air powered flying machine controlled by a pilot.[1]

The military potential of machines which have freedom of movement above the surface of the earth seems self-evident now. In the United States, the War Department was uninterested for the next three years. In Britain, establishment interest was equally dismissive of the potential of aircraft. A War Office report of 1904 recommended work only on balloons and airships. Two events, one civil and one military, changed the general appreciation of the potential of the implications of the new technology of manned aircraft. On 25 July 1909, Bleriot flew the English Channel amid worldwide publicity. The strategic security that Great Britain had enjoyed for centuries through its navy had been put in jeopardy by a fabric and piano-wire flying machine. Then in 1911, the Italians used their primitive aircraft in the war in Libya. The use of aircraft for reconnaissance was rapidly developed, and great publicity resulted from the first dropping of bombs from over the side of the aircraft.[2] In Britain, Prime Minister Asquith was concerned by the great increase in military aircraft activity overseas and he initiated a study into the implications which brought about the formation of the Royal Flying Corps in 1912. Nations absorbed the lessons at different rates and, surprisingly, the United States was amongst the slowest to invest in this new technology.[3]

Britain had sixty-three aircraft in August 1914, yet by 1918 was producing 2,000 machines every month. Military technological development accelerates rapidly under the pressure of national survival. Certainly, developments in mass production techniques were a crucial element in many areas of wartime production in 1914–18. There were considerable problems in developing both roles and equipment at a time of total war, and in meeting an enormous production requirement. Many of the modern roles of air power had been demonstrated before the war started. Torpedoes had been dropped from aircraft in 1911, and they were tested for anti-submarine operations the following year. Even deck operations from a cruiser had been tested. At the start of what was initially a land war, the role of the few aircraft involved was seen as reconnaissance, although there were still Generals who felt this was better left to the cavalry. The fighter and the bomber were both important developments during the war. The key to the fighter was the requirement for forward-facing machine-guns, while for the bomber it was accurate navigation and bombsights.

In the same way that the components for the tank were available some time before the necessary imagination to assemble them, the fighter had to wait for the interruptor mechanism that coupled the machine-gun to the aircraft. Once air-to-air combat became possible, the priority was for greater power and speed, and more firepower. The same qualities were needed for the bombers, looking for range and payload. The raids on London by German Gothas in mid-1917 were to shape strategic thinking for the inter-war period. The power to bring a war to the home population through strategic bombing was a new element in warfare.

The effect on civilian morale of a single raid by twenty-one aircraft on 7 July 1917, when some three tons of bombs were dropped on London killing sixty people, was extreme. The effect on strategic thinking, and hence on priorities for development of airpower over the next twenty years was profound. Strategists such as Douhet were already 'proving' that the bomber was the ultimate future weapon, and that wars could be won without the intervention of ground forces.[4]

In fact there were many ways in which air power could contribute to victory which were far more significant than the relatively small scale strategic raids. When the aircraft used were fully integrated with the ground forces' plans, through the co-ordinated use of reconnaissance, fire support, air defence and logistic re-supply, great results could be achieved by relatively weak forces. The Palestine campaign at the end of the World War I was a prime example of such a use of the new capabilities which airpower offered.[5] In that war, it appeared that proper exploitation of the technology was best achieved when far away from the military leadership in Europe.

Military air power went into a severe decline in the 1920s. It was expensive in capital equipment, and required highly-trained aircrew. It also lacked the strong lobby which ground and naval forces enjoyed in most countries. Indeed the establishment of a separate military arm to run air warfare was by no means universally accepted. At the end of the war, the Royal Air Force in Britain had some 22,647 aircraft, and could produce new machines at the rate of 3,500 per month. The war-winning technology was as much that of mass production as of any special weapon system. While the strategists could call for greater priority for aircraft development, nations were unwilling to divert resources to military machinery after the war to end all wars.

Technology for new military aircraft came not from the carefully-researched concepts for future wars, but from more ordinary considerations. The development of worldwide civil air travel forced the pace on aircraft design for long range, and new navigation systems. The search for higher speeds in air races, such as the Schneider trophy races of 1927-31, improved engine and airframe performances. It was the mid-1930s before the all metal monoplane became the norm. Mitchell in the United States tried to demonstrate the vulnerability of naval vessels to properly-used air-delivered weapons. However, the US Navy did begin to appreciate the importance of having their own air arm, and developing carrier-borne forces. The future of airships seemed to come to an end in this era following the R-101 and Hindenburg disasters. By the start of World War II, it

appeared that twenty years of possible technical advance had been
lost for military aircraft. The advances had come from civil aircraft
design, improved engines, better mass-production techniques and a
better understanding of aerodynamics. Communications through
radio were by now universal.

In one area of technology advance, military research was beginning
to come to fruition. In 1935, Watson-Watt in England demonstrated
the first successful aircraft detection system based on radar. Hertz
had shown in 1887 that radio waves could be reflected from solid
objects. It had taken nearly fifty years for this amusing scientific
novelty to be translated, in great secrecy, to a crucial military breakthrough. Even in this case the military application stemmed from a
Post Office report of 1932 about aircraft interfering with radio signals.[6] Other nations were also working on parallel developments but
possession by Britain gave a significant advantage in the air defence
of the country in the early stages of the war. Once the principle was
demonstrated, radar was developed in many different ways. Higher
frequencies gave greater resolution, higher power to get longer range,
smaller equipment to fit into aircraft to spot ships and submarines
on the surface. Airborne radar could be used for navigation, which
improved bombing accuracy and allowed bombing in all weathers and
at night.

The development of radar spawned a series of counter-measures
in the form of jamming and dipole metallic strips (chaff) to prevent
the target from being seen. Radar was a technical surprise of an
importance comparable to the submarine or the tank. It permitted
the aircraft to be used as an effective air defence weapon, preventing
the bomber from getting to its target. The application of science to
produce military radar parallels the development of atomic weapons.
The physical principle on which it was based was well understood,
and freely available in textbooks. It took the insight to see the military
application, coupled with the stimulus of a threat—in this case the
strategic bomber threat—to produce a research project which could
demonstrate its practicability.

World War II provided the impetus for many technical improvements to military aircraft. The bomber needed to be able to navigate
accurately to the target without visual reference, and without giving
its position away to enemy air defences. Radio navigation aids such as
Loran provided this capability. Bomb-aiming needed to be improved
through new bombsights, which coupled the benefits of improved
navigation, radar and ballistic calculations to reduce the errors.
Bombs became bigger as bombers grew larger and heavier to carry all
the equipment and self-defensive weapons. The bigger aircraft could
no longer operate from grass fields but needed concrete runways.

Thus, the technology which brought more effective bombers into being also brought a new dependence on fixed runways, which in turn became attractive targets for attack.

Fighters fitted with their own air interception radar became available from the end of 1940 onwards, and could operate effectively by night. The fighter's weapon remained the gun, but range and firepower increased as engine performance improved. Speed, rate of climb and maximum altitude all benefited from the spur which combat gave to technical progress. For air defence, the coupling of radar and anti-aircraft gun systems provided a potent combination. The problems of identification of friendly aircraft increased as air defence weapons became more capable. Again radar technology could provide an answer.

At sea, air power could be used either from land bases or from increasing numbers of aircraft carriers. The importance of the carrier to naval forces was considered in Chapter 2. Aircraft allowed firepower to be delivered at ranges far beyond earlier experience of navies. The submarine remained a difficult target, and highlighted the importance of intelligence. Indeed the work of those engaged on code-breaking was every bit as important as the new detection systems which were becoming available in the war against submarines.[7]

Towards the end of the war, there were three technological developments which were profoundly to affect air power thinking in the postwar era: the missile, the atomic bomb and the jet engine. Germany had developed two unmanned long range bombers. The V-1 was a small aircraft launched by a catapult system, powered by a pulse-jet, and guided by a gyro compass system. By designing it for a single one-way mission, no fuel for the return was needed, no aircrew had to be carried, and the ratio of warhead to overall weight was increased dramatically. The loss of self-defence capability and the inability to carry out target identification reduced the effectiveness of this weapon system. The V-2 ballistic missile overcame the vulnerability problem of the air-breathing V-1. Small unguided rockets had been developed during the war for air-to-air, anti-tank, artillery and anti-submarine use. The V-2 was a quite different weapon. It weighed 28,504lbs at launch including a one-ton warhead. All the fuel was carried internally, and it was fired to an unprecedented altitude of some seventy miles before descending ballistically towards its target. The maximum horizontal range was 200 miles, and its velocity at target was 3,500 miles per hour.[8] Here was a weapon so novel in its flight envelope that the air defences were totally impotent against it. The new technology carried penalties. Guidance was difficult, and small errors during the early powered stage led to large inaccuracies at the target. The high terminal velocity reduced effectiveness by burying the warhead too deeply. Nevertheless the V-2 pointed the way to the missile age which was to come.

The second technological breakthrough to affect the future of air power was the production of a working atomic bomb. The use of air-delivered atomic weapons at Hiroshima and Nagasaki made the strategic nuclear bomber the centrepiece of air forces' postwar development. The weight and size of the early atomic bombs made it difficult to imagine their being delivered by anything but the most powerful aircraft.

The third technological advance offered increases in power, speed and altitude through a new power source: the jet engine. So long as aircraft propulsion depended on the propeller, the aircraft would be limited by the tip speed of the blades. The principle of the jet engine was not new. A patent for a gas turbine had been issued in 1791. However it took developments in materials to provide components which could be machined with precision and yet withstand the very high temperatures and stresses. The Whittle patent for a gas turbine aircraft engine was published in 1930. Yet the subsequent development was remarkably slow. The first jet aircraft, the Heinkel He 176, flew in 1939 yet it was 1944 before the first jet fighters were used in combat. As the power available from jet engines has increased and designers have sought greater performance from aircraft, the manufacturing tolerances of every part have become more critical. Greater understanding of aerodynamics has improved performance yet further. The sound barrier proved to be conquerable and supersonic aircraft developed. The penalty associated with increased performance was one of cost and fuel consumption.

In looking at the development of aerospace power since 1945, it is possible to argue that there have been enormous technological advances which were impossible to foresee; yet at the same time the application of technology to countermeasures has negated many of the enhancements. The one result from technological progress has been rapidly increasing unit costs of aircraft. Considering each of the roles which air power plays in modern warfare, it is possible to determine where technology has significantly enhanced capability.

The earliest use of the air was for reconnaissance and that remains a vital part of military capability today. The jet aircraft allowed higher altitudes to give greater coverage, and slant viewing from safe territory. The vulnerability of high flying aircraft to modern air defence systems has reduced their effectiveness near hostile airspace, but they may be the only method of obtaining rapid large-scale survey information. This strategic reconnaissance can also be obtained from satellite-based systems. The successful placing into orbit of Sputnik I in 1957 heralded a technological development which has had many implications for future wars. The reconnaissance information available from the wide range of sensors in space provides much better overall coverage than would be available from aircraft. There still remains an important role for the reconnaissance aircraft when specific areas need to be studied, and also in the tactical situation. In the latter, the aircraft is likely to be flying at very low level, at high subsonic speed, and using visual, infra-red and radar sensors. In this respect it is an evolutionary development from the photo-recce aircraft of the last war. There is, however, one form of air reconnaissance which does represent a new power. This is the airborne early warning aircraft carrying powerful radar systems, and the associated data-processing capability which allows it to act as a flying radar station which can control an air battle.

The bomber has also evolved in the intervening years. The evolution has not been as dramatic as is characterized by the high technology appearance of the modern supersonic bomber. While high speed and high altitude seemed important qualities in the early days of the nuclear jet aircraft, air defences have forced the bomber to very low-level operations. The problems of terrain avoidance and fuel consumption at these heights have effectively limited speeds to the high subsonic region. A comparison between the Lancaster bomber of World War II and today's Tornado is illuminating. The Lancaster flying at medium altitude could carry much the same bomb load over nearly twice the distance as the Tornado, which flies at just over twice the speed on an operational sortie. It took a crew of seven to operate the Lancaster, against the Tornado's two-man team, and it cost just £45,000 in 1945. Taking normal price inflation into account, a Tornado costs twenty times the 1985 cost of a Lancaster. This crude comparison of speed, bomb load and combat radius hides the transformation in the operational environment over the forty years. The Lancaster could not reach the target against the modern air defence systems, and the high cost of the modern offensive aircraft reflects the necessity of the technological fixes to improve its survivability. The technology also increases effectiveness through all-weather operation and greater accuracy of weapon delivery. The price of this technology reduces the total number of aircraft available. The balance between these two factors will determine whether offensive air power is of increasing or diminishing importance in future wars.

One area in offensive air operations where technology has been relatively slow to provide new capabilities has been in the weapons themselves. Conventional bombs have developed relatively slowly. The major thrust has been towards greater accuracy in delivery through some form of guidance. Laser target marking has allowed precision-bombing when conditions permit the designation of the target. Design of bombs specific to targets has been slow in coming, but for anti-airfield use specialist munitions are now entering service. The unit costs of such weapons are significantly greater than those of the dumb iron bombs.

The primacy of the strategic bomber for nuclear deterrence was lost in the 1960s as the ballistic missile became a much more certain way of delivering nuclear weapons to strategic targets. The coupling of nuclear weapons to ballistic missiles has been the major technological achievement of the postwar era. Mutual deterrence depends on an assured nuclear retaliatory capability, and the wide variety of nuclear systems available provide this. The development of multiple warheads for these missiles, different basing methods, and cruise as well as ballistic delivery, have made the retaliatory capability even more assured and have reinforced deterrence. Guidance systems have improved to the extent that singular military targets can be held at risk as well as area economic targets.

Moving to air defence, the development of the air defence missile has transformed the way in which aircraft must operate. Missiles can be guided visually, by radar and through heat-seeking sensors. All these guidance systems work in straight lines, and if located on the ground will have a minimum effective altitude. This gives a higher chance of survivability to the low flying aircraft, although they will remain vulnerable to modern fighters looking down on them. An alternative countermeasure is to fool the air defence sensor system through jamming or deception. The developments in electronics have made this an area of much greater importance in modern warfare. Fighters have changed significantly in effectiveness: in contrast to their close range operation of guns in 1940, the modern fighter need never see its target. Long-range radar allows an enemy aircraft to be destroyed with air-to-air missiles at extended ranges. More than one target can be engaged simultaneously, and the fighter can remain on airborne alert for long periods through air-to-air refuelling. The cost of the modern fighter has increased by even more than the bomber. The increased capability to defend against enemy aircraft is limited by the difficulties in positively identifying distant targets as hostile or friendly. Technology has yet to provide a satisfactory unambiguous solution to this problem.

The postwar period has seen technology enhancing the ability for offensive aircraft to penetrate to their targets, and at the same time for defensive systems to prevent that penetration. The consensus view appears to be that the defensive systems are winning in this technological battle. Future aircraft are unlikely to be able to penetrate close to heavily-defended targets, and will depend increasingly on weapons which can be fired at a distance from the target. These types of stand-off weapons are now being developed, and are considered further in Chapter 15.

Looking next at the developments in air transport, the first major crisis after World War II showed, through the Berlin airlift, the strategic nature of massive airlift capability. Almost without noticing, the comparatively lower technology of the transport aircraft has brought a new concept to military force. Governments have been able to shape defence policies around their ability to deploy forces by air to remote trouble spots. The large carrying capability, coupled with in-flight refuelling, has made reinforcement over thousands of miles possible in a matter of hours.

Maritime aircraft have benefited from the improvements in navigation equipment, carrying capability, range and stand-off weapon systems. In terms of a breakthrough in ability to detect and destroy submarines, the process remains as much an art as a science. Technology has provided novel aids which can detect magnetic anomalies, relay acoustic information, and enhance all the sensor information, collate it and display it. The submarine which wishes to stay hidden still has the advantage.

In aircraft design, a major change has been the move away from dependence on increasingly vulnerable runways. As aircraft became bigger and more complex, their requirements for prepared take-off and landing surfaces became more demanding. This made airfields attractive targets to reduce enemy air effort. In many cases airfields may not be conveniently located. Two developments have made certain aspects of air power independent of runways. The first was the helicopter. First used in the Korean war, it was a rescue and medical evacuation vehicle. Experience in the Vietnam war showed how versatile the helicopter could be for reconnaissance, command and control, transport, and as a firepower platform. Helicopters are now fitted with a range of armament for close air support roles, and have a rapidly growing place in nations' inventories. Technology has improved the lift capability, the handling characteristics and the weapons available. The vulnerability of a relatively slow-moving and fragile aircraft remains a problem. Nevertheless, there are those who would argue that the armed helicopter is the tank's successor, and the cargo helicopter can replace the armoured personnel carrier. This would make the ground forces more mobile and less easy to obstruct. A judgement of whether cost and vulnerability will be the limiting factors will have to await more combat experience.

The second method of removing dependence on runways has been the development of fixed-wing aircraft with vertical take-off and landing (VTOL) capability. What at first seemed an innovation of limited application has now been proved through the contribution the Harrier was able to make in the Falklands conflict of 1982. The flexibility offered by such a high performance aircraft operating from dispersed field sites, or from small ships, has not been taken up as widely as might have been expected. There are logistic support and aircraft performance penalties associated with VTOL operations. However under some circumstances it may be the only way of operating.

For military vehicles operating in the earth's atmosphere, there have been surprisingly few major changes in concepts since World War II. The advent of the air defence missile has forced the pace of countermeasures. Aircraft fly lower and faster, but no further than before. The maximum possible speeds and altitudes are no longer sought after. While demands for operating bases grew more stringent initially as aircraft became more complex, technology has been moving towards reducing such dependence. Apart from helicopter operations, concepts for the use of air power today are not very different from those of forty years ago. Technology has improved capabilities, but the battle remains the same.

Since 1957, the regions beyond the earth's atmosphere have assumed increasing importance to national security. Technology has made space the extended battlefield. It is possible to argue that the military uses of space have developed at a remarkably slow pace. While larger payloads have been placed in orbit, and modern electronics and computer technology allows much more capability to be given to any payload, the costs of space systems remain extraordinarily high. In the first three decades of this century aircraft moved from the Wright Flyer to a worldwide use of aircraft for offensive, defensive, reconnaissance and transport. In the thirty years since Sputnik I was placed in orbit, progress has been much less dramatic. The use of satellites has assumed increasing importance for reconnaissance, communication and navigation. The ability to launch such systems remains in the hands of very few nations.

Military reconnaissance satellites are used for photographic survey, electronic information-gathering, missile early warning, meteorological data-gathering and for geodetic measurements for missile targeting. These all represent quite new capabilities in the scale of information which can be collected. Military communications are becoming increasingly dependent on satellite relay. While long-range communication has been possible through HF radio, propagation has at times been unpredictable and data density was limited. Communications satellites offer comprehensive high density communications over very great distances, and allow control to be retained at much higher levels than before. Satellite-based navigation systems allow military systems to fix their positions to unprecedented degrees of accuracy, with significant implications for weapon delivery accuracies.

In these rather limited ways space technology has added to military capability. The cost of the systems is high, and the reliability of launch systems remains less than perfect. Satellites are extremely vulnerable to a number of countermeasures. By their nature they are in exposed positions, which are easily located. The Soviet Union has tested an anti-satellite weapon system based on an exploding satellite. The United States is developing an anti-satellite missile. Some reconnaissance sensors may be vulnerable to damage by high-energy laser directed at them from the earth. Technology has provided, at a high cost, space-based systems which become increasingly relied upon for command, control, communication and information. Yet the capability is also a vulnerability if anti-satellite systems are being developed. The further potential for the military uses of space are explored in Chapter 8.

Since the beginning of the twentieth century technology has made air power, and latterly aerospace power, of increasing importance. The ability to move away from the restrictions of movement on the earth's surface offers a new arena for military conflict. The lessons of the past suggest that our predecessors found it difficult to make the right development decisions in a timely way. Extrapolations of limited combat data resulted in false strategic concepts. With the benefit of hindsight, the technological developments which have crucially affected aerospace warfare are the invention of the aircraft, radar, nuclear weapons, and the missile. It may be that the future historian will place the helicopter/VTOL aircraft or satellites among these milestones. Alternatively their vulnerability may mark them down with the airships of the past.

The characteristics of the four major technological areas may give some direction to thinking about future possibilities. The aircraft offered a new scale for firepower in both range of action and speed of reaction. It gave a new flexibility to the use of military force, which could be applied to a whole range of widely-separated targets. Radar made the invisible visible. The vast regions of the sky or the sea could be explored at the speed of light, and appropriate countermeasures taken. Nuclear weapons provide destructive power on a scale previously unimagined. Indeed with thermonuclear weapons, the energy released was virtually unlimited. The potential damage from even a single weapon has changed the whole nature of international relations. Finally the missile has provided an unstoppable delivery method for the nuclear weapon. As we examine the opportunities for the future, the relative effectiveness of the manned aircraft against the missile will need close scrutiny. The future applications of space technology will also need to be examined. Aerospace technology grows ever more expensive, and yet concepts have not made dramatic changes.

Research in many areas will have much to offer the military in the future. In the Chapters which follow, we examine the prospects in eight different fields of investigation.

Part Two – Science Today

CHAPTER 5

High Energy Physics

THERE IS something slightly bizarre in the prospect of the smallest fundamental particles of matter being employed to destroy the most powerful weapons which man can build. Modern physics has been a story akin to the opening of an endless series of Russian dolls. The discovery of the atomic nature of matter at the start of the last century was an immensely important achievement. John Dalton's experiments on the chemical composition of compounds revealed that there were atomic building blocks, from which all substances derived. The ordering of the elements into a structured table by Mendeléev in 1869, where properties could be predicted and missing elements identified, gave great confidence to scientists that they had discovered the true nature of matter. But the very predictability of the elements when tabulated by their atomic weight suggested some finer structure to their composition. This century, the structure of the atom has been explored. Initially it seemed relatively simple. The less than 100 elements could be explained by suitable combinations of smaller building blocks: electrons, protons and neutrons. In recent years the number of these sub-atomic particles which have been identified has grown until they are as numerous as the elements. The simple triad of particles has been joined by the neutrino, photon, muon, pion, kaon and many others. Just as the periodic table of the middle of the last century made it possible to predict undiscovered elements, so the start of attempts to classify the sub-atomic particles has led to prediction and discovery of previously unknown particles. This in turn has led to attempts to look for some fine structure to the elementary particles, and the search for quarks—the building blocks of sub-atomic particles.[1]

All this pure physics research has required higher and higher energy particle accelerators to investigate the fundamental nature of matter. Indeed, the term 'particle' is no more than a convenient label for the reader. The physicists are not investigating particles in the sense of grains of sand, but are measuring phenomena which can be identified by mass and energy level, and effects on other 'particles'. In the search for simplicity of cause, atomic theory led to the identifi-

44

cation of more than 100 elements, and many, many isotopes of those atoms. The simple structure underlying the atoms has grown more complex until there are more than 100 sub-atomic particles. The investigations of the physicists have shown that in controlling the interaction of matter there seem to be only four types of force. Gravity is the one which affects us in the normal world, but it is remarkably weak compared to the other fundamental forces. The others are the electromagnetic force, the weak nuclear force and the strong nuclear force. Investigations into the nature of these forces has also required bigger and bigger accelerators and the science of high energy physics is one of the major international areas of collaboration because of the high costs of the equipment involved. Research must be devoted into the design of the accelerators and into the power sources for them.[2]

One other major area for research into this field is in the search for fusion power. While current atomic energy is derived from the radioactive decay of atoms, this, in nuclear terms, releases only a small proportion of the energy locked in the nuclear structure. Our sun is able to burn for millions of years by fusing light atoms into heavier ones and releasing much greater amounts of fusion energy. In order to generate the necessary conditions for atomic fusion, a concentration of very high energy particles must be achieved. The necessary energy levels at sufficient concentrations have so far only been achieved for long enough in the middle of an atomic bomb. The atomic fission explosion provides the firelighter for the fusion process in thermonuclear weapons. A great deal of civil research effort is being expended on the search for a way to produce the necessary conditions in a more controlled way through accelerated particles confined in magnetic bottles. This line of civil energy research brings more expertise to bear on the problems of producing very high energy particle beams, and also the control of those beams to precise criteria.[3]

One other area of high energy physics research which has implications for military use is that of laser research. The laser was initially an interesting demonstration of the discrete nature of energy states in matter. Changes from one energy state to another in an atom are accompanied by emission or absorption of radiation. The discreteness of the energy states is characterized by the associated radiation being of a single frequency. Just as a small sound picked up by a microphone near to a loudspeaker builds up to a loud squeal of feedback, so a small pulse of light reflected back into the laser material produces an amplification of the radiation through further emission, which produces in turn an intense 'squeal' of laser light. The light, or other radiation, produced has curious properties.[4] It is coherent in nature. As a result of its being produced at a single frequency, with all the waves in step with one another, the beam spreads very little with distance, and can be focused to give intense energy concentrations. While initially a scientific novelty, the increasing power of lasers has made them important tools in investigating the nature of matter, as well as an increasing number of industrial applications.

In the military field, high energy particle beams and high energy lasers offer the prospect of a new class of firepower: directed energy weapons. Science fiction writers have been attracted to the prospect of instantaneous death rays for years. This does not mean that they necessarily offer any advantages over the more mundane methods of destruction. For directed energy to offer a useful avenue for military research, the advantages must be demonstrable given the high costs of high energy physics research. Can directed energy weapons offer the prospect of changing the nature of warfare in the same sense as the repeating rifle, the aircraft, the submarine or the atomic weapon?

In three areas the use of directed energy weapons appears to offer new opportunities:

(a) *Speed of delivery*. Laser radiation travels at the speed of light, and particle beams can be accelerated to significant fractions of the speed of light. Thus time of flight problems of more physical missiles are eliminated. Aiming at moving targets becomes much simpler. Damage can be assessed and if necessary the target re-engaged, where it might have passed beyond the operational range of missile or gun.

(b) *Range*. The range of a laser beam is theoretically infinite in a vacuum. Despite the coherence of the radiation, it does diverge and the power per unit area decreases with distance. The ability to focus the beam helps, and operational ranges of 1,000km in space are conceivable in the future. The effective range of particle beams is a complex issue, which is discussed further below.

(c) *Logistics*. At first inspection, the use of massless photons of light, or streams of protons, in place of heavy shells or missiles seem to solve the logistic supply problem of modern warfare at a stroke. Unfortunately, the energy requirements must be met from some fuel sources and the overall logistic bill must be considered carefully in any proposed system.

These three factors are sufficiently important for serious consideration to be given to the role of directed energy weapons in future warfare. But before deciding on their deployment, the physical constraints on their operations must also be examined. Particle beams can be of two types: charged—using electrons or protons; or neutral—using neutrons or hydrogen atoms. An electron beam system is commonplace in the home today. The television cathode ray tube is a particle beam accelerator. Electrons are produced from a heated filament, are accelerated by high voltage plates, and manipulated by electric and magnetic fields to produce a focused beam on the surface of the television screen. Typically the electrons are accelerated through a voltage of a few thousand volts, and are equivalent to a current flow measured in microamps. The enormous research particle accelerators can achieve very high kinetic energies. Protons are accelerated to 500,000 million electron volts (500 GeV) in the gigantic circular Fermi accelerator. The power of such a beam is the product of their energy and the number of particles produced per second. Just as a car light bulb operating at 12 volts and using 2 amps has a power of $2 \times 12 = 24$ watts, so our 1,000 GeV accelerator with a current of 0.6 milliamps has a power of 600 megawatts. Research into fusion reactors has produced high current particle beams but at much lower energies. The power of a useful beam weapon would require particles accelerated to the order of 1 GeV at currents of 1,000 amps sustained for 0.1 of a millisecond. This represents a power of a million megawatts. No such accelerator is yet available.[5]

While the power requirements for particle beam weapons are daunting, the nature of the beam itself is also an area of uncertainty. Charged particles can be relatively easily accelerated and focused into a beam. However once in free flight, the repulsion between similar charged bodies causes the beam to disperse. An electron beam 1cm wide as it leaves the accelerator has spread to some 15 metres across at a range of 1,000 kms; and a similar proton beam would be 18 kms wide. Beam dispersion of that size makes the optimistic assumption that the path is in free space without an external magnetic field. A charged particle beam travelling in the atmosphere or in the earth's magnetic field would be dispersed or deflected to an extent which would make long-range use impossible. The use of neutrally-charged particle beams would overcome both the electrical and magnetic deflection effects, but brings with it new problems. The particles must start with an electrical charge, so that they can be accelerated and focused. Then the beam must be neutralized, which causes some spreading which continues to increase with distance. At a nominal 1,000km a neutral beam might be expected to have diverged to about 20 metres across, assuming that the source charged particle beam could be kept focused to an accuracy of one part in a million.

Our theoretical particle beam weapon would aim to produce sufficiently energetic particles at the target to penetrate its protective outer layer, and in sufficient concentration to damage the internal electronics or even detonate any high explosive warhead. The propagation difficulties are at their least in space and so particle beam weapons seem to offer attractions for anti-ballistic missile and anti-satellite systems. However the sheer size of the accelerators and the prodigious power requirements, coupled with the precise control needed in an unpredictable magnetic environment, makes the particle beam weapon in space based on current developments unlikely to be a productive avenue of research. In the atmosphere, propagation over relatively short distances may be possible by boring an evacuated channel in the air with a high power laser, before sending the particle beam down it. This might have applications for the short-range interception of incoming missiles. It is comparable to firing a tank gun through a brick wall so that you can fire a bullet through the resulting hole. If a high power laser can produce such a controllable effect, then it can be used as the weapon itself.

At the current stage of research into accelerated particle beams, their application as weapons seems remote. They could provide destructive firepower, but at considerably greater cost than more conventional means. There are also a number of relatively low cost countermeasures which can be taken to disperse the beam before it strikes the target, or reduce the effect if it does strike home. This is not to say that at some stage in the future, particle beams may not have a role to play. Fortunately there are so many industrial and pure physics research projects driving the development of particle beam accelerators, that work will continue apace without needing military prompting. If power requirements, focusing and control mechanisms, propagation characteristics and the physical size of the equipment change dramatically under civilian development, then it will be time for military applications to be reviewed. Until then particle beam weapons offer little save novelty to defence.

The laser does not suffer from the magnetic and electric dispersion problems of particle beams. Widespread publicity has accompanied the testing of high energy lasers against drones. It is already possible to provide sufficient energy in a laser beam at short range to destroy a military target in clear atmospheric conditions. This does not necessarily mean that the laser is the best way to destroy such targets. A surface-to-air missile, or a radar-laid anti-aircraft gun can also do the job. Any laser weapon would be different in nature from other weapons. Its destructive power would be in the form of electromagnetic radiation. It would deliver its destruction at the speed of light, some 300 million metres per second or 100,000 times faster than a missile. It must also be aimed to strike the target, and held on the target for long enough to cause the necessary damage. In the atmosphere, the power of the laser beam is limited by the electrical breakdown of the air at high energy concentrations. It is also attenuated by dust, smoke, cloud or any medium which obscures radiation at that wavelength. While the classic demonstrations of lasers burning holes in razor blades suggest a mechanism for destruction of targets based on melting, this is unlikely to be the most efficient use. By pulsing the laser into high energy bursts of radiation, it is possible to cause damage to target aircraft or missiles by cracking. If the pulse rate is high enough, the thermal effect assists the fracturing process. This process is helped when the target material is already under stress, as it would be in a missile in flight. In the atmosphere, the range would be limited both by the atmospheric conditions and the power density limitations. In space, these limitations are relaxed while the necessary ranges are increased dramatically. Now the constraints become design problems for generating and focusing the necessary laser power.

The laser is already a useful military tool. Low power lasers are widely used on the battlefield. As a rangefinger, the laser provides instantaneous and accurate information for weapon aiming calculations. This task can be done by optical or radar sighting methods, but the laser gives much more precise measurements and is much less prone to enemy countermeasures. It is possible to conceive of further developments in this area leading towards a laser-based radar system. A relatively low power laser with a scanning mirror, coupled to an electro-optical detection system could provide a precise three-dimensional picture of target location, with far greater discrimination of detail than radar. It could be more difficult to detect and jam given the availability of tunable lasers and filters. The overwhelming disadvantage of such a system would be the problems of propagation in obscured atmospheric conditions. However, developments in higher frequency lasers in the ultra-violet and beyond regions of the electromagnetic spectrum may bring new possibilities in this application.

One particular such application has already been considered. The oceans currently provide an excellent obscuring medium for military covert activities. The detection of submarines is still as much an art as a science. The oceans are vast hiding places, with the propagation of both sound and electromagnetic radiation subject to anomalies as the waves pass through the differing layers of water. Nevertheless, it has been reported that laser interferometry has been successfully used to detect submarines.[6] Given the importance of strategic submarine detection to superpower nuclear retaliatory capability, this will be an area of intense research activity. If a laser, which could make the oceans transparent, could be mounted on a reconnaissance satellite, strategic stability could be radically altered. The propagation of electromagnetic radiation in water gives little prospect for the achievement of this aim. However, the significance of any technical breakthrough means that this is an area where continuing research is essential.

The laser is widely used today as a target designator for precision-guided munitions. If a target can be illuminated by a beam of laser light, a missile or shell with a relatively low-cost terminal guidance system can home on to the characteristic illuminated spot, and hit the target accurately. This has great attractions to the soldier. The difficulties in passing instructions from the front line to the close air support aircraft or the fire support artillery battery are overcome. The general area of the target is sufficient, provided that the target is marked by the hand-held laser. It can also be used by the weapon operator as an alternative means of guidance to control wire, radio beam or radar. The system is well proven, and future development work is needed in improving the method of designation. Currently, the laser operator must be within line of sight of the target, which is by definition a somewhat vulnerable location, whether from the ground or in the air. It is likely that these target designation tasks will be possible from cheap unmanned Remotely Piloted Vehicles (RPVs) in the future. The operator can be located safely to the rear of the action, select targets from information relayed by the RPV, and lock the laser illuminator on target. Artillery, surface-to-surface or air-to-ground missiles can then home in on the illuminated target. The advantages with such an approach are that the lowest cost items are placed at greatest risk, where the high cost men and machines have reduced exposure to the enemy, while the high kill rates of precision-guided munitions are achieved.

Lasers are also in use as means of communication. The electromagnetic radiation in a laser beam is different from a radio wave only in being of higher frequency. The information capacity which a radio wave can carry depends on its frequency. The higher the frequency the more information, in the form of communication channels, which can be carried. The tight beam of a laser is also far more difficult to interfere with through jamming. While a piece of thin card placed between the beam would stop communication, placing the card is far more difficult than the blanket high power radio jamming which is possible. In the same way, there is no spillover of radiation which can be detected, used for intelligence or position-finding. The disadvantages of modulated laser communication systems are those of the propagation of lasers in the atmosphere. This can be overcome by the use of fibre optics which pipe the light with much less attenuation, just as a wire can carry telephone communication. In looking at communication on the future battlefield, a system which was proof against the hostile electronic warfare environment would be a great asset. The technical problems of using lasers are considerable for mobile manpack systems. Yet low-cost relay masts with automatic orientation might offer possibilities. At sea, data transmission by such means might offer advantages, and relay through satellite retransmission could offer great flexibility.

One other current offshoot of the laser will certainly have some military applications. The coherent predictable nature of laser light allows photographs to be taken, which can reconstruct the original waveforms when re-illuminated by a laser. The holograms produced are three-dimensional pictures in a true sense, in that a photographed object can be viewed from different positions. While current applications seem more artistic than scientific, the possibility of much more realistic simulation and instrumentation through holographic processes will bring the laser into another area of military development.

Moving away from the low powered laser and into more powerful offensive use of laser weapons, power levels for damage to the human eye and to optical sensors are relatively easy to achieve. Blinding the pilot of a modern aircraft through a laser eye damage weapon would be an effective method of destroying the aircraft. However, it is not as simple as might at first be thought. The laser which is focused by the lens in the eye on to the retina, must be powerful enough to burn the retina over the time the beam is held on target. The target is remarkably small compared to the aircraft, and is obscured by the aircraft canopy and the pilot's visor. Given also the propagation problems of lasers in the smoke of the battlefield, the laser eye damage weapon is unlikely to be worth developing as a primary air defence system. A more useful approach is to accept the effect as a bonus for other defensive systems. If an air defence gun is fitted with a laser rangefinder, then it may be worth increasing the power levels so that eye damage becomes possible. This will force the opposition into taking protective measures which will degrade the overall mission effectiveness. The same line of argument holds for damaging sensor systems, particularly fitted to aircraft.

One class of sensors do offer opportunities for laser countermeasures. These are the reconnaissance satellites. Predictable targets free from the problems of the atmosphere and with extremely sensitive sensors are particularly vulnerable to laser damage. Such damage can be covert, as the satellite will continue to orbit while blinded. The offensive laser could be earth-based, aircraft-borne or deployed in space. Since the sensors are likely to be orientated towards the earth beneath, the target area for the reconnaissance is also the best area for deployment of the offensive laser. Use of a high-flying aircraft with such a system allows considerable flexibility, and reduces the atmospheric absorption problems. Such systems would appear to have considerable potential.

Looking to yet higher powers for lasers, the target set is similar to that considered in the analysis of the prospects for particle beam weapons. Satellites, missiles and aircraft are the prime candidates for an operational laser weapon system. The problems of propagation in obscured atmospheric conditions would make the laser an unreliable weapon. If the weather has to be fine, and smoke can obscure not just vision but also killing power, then the laser is unlikely to become the ray gun of tomorrow's infantry. While the photons in the beam may be massless, the equipment necessary to generate the power and the fuel to provide the energy both have traditional logistic penalties. Basing laser weapons in space has great attractions in allowing long-distance propagation with little attentuation. The power generation and fuel requirements become even more difficult to achieve. One analysis[7] concluded that it would take 125 years to deliver the fuel necessary for a laser weapon system designed to cope with the Soviet ICBM threat. The study pointed out that the laser power necessary was beyond technical possibility currently. A lesser problem would be a laser system to destroy satellites. Given that a space-based system would itself be vulnerable to a similar enemy system, an aircraft-carried system would again have attractions. The copious writings[8] on complex laser weapons using enormous mirrors in space have yet to show them to be attractive options. While the problems of weight and size of power supplies, and the fuel requirements, could be overcome by a ground-fixed laser site focused on a space mirror, the increasing number of critical points also increases the overall vulnerability of such a weapon system.

Looking to yet more powerful lasers of the future,[9] research continues into higher frequency and greater power regions. Chemical lasers, using hydrogen or deuterium and fluorine as fuels, have been reported as achieving outputs greater than one megawatt, but that is likely to be the limit. Excimer krypton-fluoride lasers are higher frequency but still four orders of magnitude below power requirements for ballistic missile defence systems. Free electron lasers have the advantage of being tunable so that the best frequency for propagation can be chosen, but the high powers come at the lower frequencies. This can be used to advantage as a high-power radio frequency weapon, by using microwave energy to disrupt communications systems or cause local heating.[10] The X-ray laser using a nuclear explosion as the source of energy is one possible avenue.[11] While this might overcome some of the problems of sheer mass of fuel supplies in space, it introduces new difficulties. The large number of potential targets in any ballistic missile defence make a weapon which self-destructs with a nuclear explosion each time it is fired an expensive option. Indeed the precise aiming required might well be difficult to achieve under such circumstances.

Lasers offer less exciting prospects for future weapon systems than many would suggest. As components of various systems, they will be increasingly used for the unique characteristics which coherent radiation offers. They are already in use for communication, weapon aiming and target marking. With little extra development they could add eye damage and sensor damage capabilities. As high-energy destructive weapons, the physical limitations associated with beam generation is likely to restrict them to relatively few target types. Satellites may be the most vulnerable laser weapon targets, and the weapon would be best operated from high flying aircraft. Just as civil research into particle beams will ensure that technological surprise is unlikely to be achieved by a potential enemy, so it is with laser research. The industrial and domestic use of lasers from the compact disc player to the laser fusion reactor will keep research going. More military applications will undoubtedly be found, but many will emerge from civil research projects rather than dedicated military research.

CHAPTER 6

Computing Science

COMPUTATION has been a vital aspect of military science for many years. Among the early requirements were the need for ballistic tables, navigational and also astronomical techniques. Today, individuals have immense computational power readily available and computers have an impact on all aspects of life. In examining the military prospects for future developments in computer science it is necessary to chart the recent exponential rise in capabilities and identify the forces, both military and civil, which have powered the developments.

While the tasks demanded of computational devices range from displaying the time on a clock to predicting worldwide weather patterns, there are a number of common features to all today's systems. A computer takes in information and instructions, stores this data, processes the information according to the instructions and then feeds out the processed data. The system may be as apparently simple as the pocket calculator. Here the information is fed in through the keyboard as numerical data and mathematical operations. The calculator stores the numbers and processes them according to the requirements of the mathematical function. It then feeds out the numerical result to the display. Or it may be a jet engine fuel control system; here the information will come from many temperature, pressure and control sensors. It will be processed according to preplanned instructions and the output will be in the form of electro-mechanical control of the fuel system.

The route to the small, powerful, cheap computing device starts from the military pressures of World War II. In 1944, J. Presper Eckert Jr and John W. Mauchly were developing a machine to compute artillery tables for the US army. This machine, the Electronic Numerical Integrator and Computer (ENIAC) was completed in 1945; it could complete 5,000 additions per second, and could do in a day calculations which would take a man six years. The major drawback was that the sequence of calculations had to be wired in, and altering the sequence was therefore a complicated undertaking. The computational power would have been of great help to another military project. The scientists working on the atomic bomb project at Los Alamos were having to complete long and vital calculations with mechanical calculators and paper and pencil. One of them, John von Neumann, saw the possibilities of developing the ENIAC-type machine so that the sequence of operations could be changed through the use of stored instructions instead of rewiring. His ideas were not ready in time to help the scientists on the Manhattan Project, but it was the catalyst of two military needs which brought the ideas together which led to the programmable electronic computer. In a paper in 1945,[1] von Neumann described the building blocks for the modern computer.

Following the war, research continued in the universities and the commercial possibilities added impetus to the development work. The first large commercially available computer systems appeared in 1951 in the form of the Ferranti and the Univac models. Since that time, power and reliability have increased by many orders of magnitude, while cost and size has decreased radically. This had led to a proliferation in applications of computing devices comparable only perhaps to the spread of machine-tools in the last century. Today computers will be found everywhere. Even the average home will have them in clocks, television sets, heating controls, cookers, washing machines, toys, cars, typewriters and video recorders, apart from the more obvious calculators and personal computers. How has a machine like ENIAC,[2] with some 19,000 valves, 1,500 relays, hundreds of thousands of resistors, capacitors and inductors, housed in a large air-conditioned room, and consuming 200kw of electricity been reduced to the size of a pack of cards, able to run off a torch battery, and all for the price of a book?

Looking first at the most obvious reason, there have been two developments in electronics which have led to significant miniaturization. The early electronic computers depended on thermionic valves, which were inherently bulky, power-intensive and unreliable. The invention in 1948 of the transistor, a solid state switching and amplifying device, offered a much smaller component which needed no power to run heated filaments. Difficulty in developing reliable mass production techniques, and perhaps also a lack of foresight of either military or civil users, meant that it was 1963 before the first transistor desk calculator was in production. By this time the pressures of space technology and the missile developments were generating much more interest in miniaturization of electronic components in general, and computers in particular. Individual component size reduced, and the use of printed circuit boards reduced circuit sizes somewhat. From there the idea of etching the transistor—or more than one—with its associated components, on to single pieces of suitably treated semiconductor was developed. The integrated circuit became the successor to the transistor. The driving force of the missile and satellite programmes increased the packing density of components. Since 1959 the number of elements contained in each integrated circuit has doubled annually. Once the power, reliability and widespread application of these devices became apparent, commercial development led to mass production techniques and reduced costs. The production techniques have been further improved by computer-aided design: the power of the modern computer is harnessed to make even more powerful computers.

Can these trends of greater component density at less cost continue for ever? There are a number of physical limitations. Individual component size is now down to fractions of a micron. That is a size of the order of the wavelength of light. It is not, therefore, possible to use light to 'draw' the components. X-rays or electron beams provide the shorter wavelengths necessary to focus and draw some fine detail. The packing density will therefore be limited by the technology available to manufacture the integrated circuits. As the system moves into the high energy physics régime costs are also likely to rise. Another concern is that as size of components decrease to atomic-like dimensions, quantum effects become significant, and the predictability of operations may decrease. In one analysis of the fundamental physical limits of computation[3] the authors assert that the uncertainty principle need not theoretically constrain computer capability. Other constraints arrive as numbers of components increase. The time that information takes to travel is limited by the speed of light, and processing time is also a limiting factor. We shall examine potentially-useful techniques for increasing power per unit volume later in this Chapter.

The advances in integrated circuits have allowed the production of the computer on a chip; that is all the components necessary to accept input of data and instructions, a store for the information, a processing unit and an output of the processed information. The storage of data has seen a similarly spectacular decrease in size. Early computers depended on punched cards or paper tapes for the input of data, and bulky delay lines or magnetic drums for temporary storage of data within the computer. These gave way in the 1960s to magnetic tape input and output of data, with the computers using magnetic core memory for its internal operations. The drawbacks of the sequential nature of data stored on tape have since been overcome by the use of magnetic disc systems which can be accessed at any point. Internal memory has been taken over by integrated circuits giving large arrays of switches. We have moved from the punched card which could hold 80 bytes of information to the hard disc which can hold 500 million bytes. For internal memory, the delay line of the early computers was some 5ft long and could hold around 1,000 bits with an access time measured in milliseconds. Today, the solid state Random Access Memory can hold a quarter of a million bits on a chip measuring less than an inch square, with an access time of a fraction of a microsecond.

Today, the most powerful computers are designed to minimize the time taken for signals to travel within the machine, and speed of operation is measured in megaflops. A megaflop is one million floating point operations per second. At its peak, the Cyber 205 used for weather forecasting can achieve speeds of 400 megaflops.[4] The speed at which the signal pulses travel through the wires connecting the various components of the computer is of the order of 15cms. per nanosecond. Despite the advances in miniaturization through the development of Ultra Large Scale Integration (USLI: the manufacture of over one million components on a single chip), a powerful computer needs large amounts of memory. While individual integrated circuits can be designed with cycle times of one nanosecond, the physical size of the Cyber 205 increases the minimum cycle time for the machine to 12.5 nanoseconds.[5] To make further progress in improving speed of operation, the intercomponent distances will need to be reduced to a configuration where operations are not constrained by the time it takes for the signals to travel. Not only does this present severe manufacturing difficulties, the problem of heat dissipation becomes critical. It is likely, therefore, that advances will come now from new approaches to the problem.

One technique has been the use of many relatively simple processors connected in such a way that they work simultaneously on a problem with their own dedicated memory. One such working parallel computer, using 65,536 simple parallel processors, averages some 2,500 megaflops.[6] Theoretically such a design system could be used to produce a computer with a thousand million parallel processors. Using current technology it would be as large as a building, cost twenty times as much as the largest commercial computer, but be able to carry out 100 million million instructions per second. Such a system requires quite different approaches to problem-solving, so that the operations can be processed in parallel rather than sequentially.[7] This may be the limiting area, and the research on software development may become more critical than novelty in the computer hardware.

It may be that the semiconductor junction, which has held sway since the transistor, has run its course, as the thermionic valve did before it. Different switch devices are already available. The Josephson junction depends on quantum-mechanical effects displayed by thin insulating layers at temperatures near absolute zero. A junction can be arranged which is superconducting until a magnetic field is applied when it switches to being resistive. The switching time between the two states can be as low as six picoseconds (6×10^{-12} secs), and the power consumption is very small. A superconducting computer with an overall cycle time of two nanoseconds could be constructed in a two-inch cube.[8] Another switch offering low power consumption, high speed and high component density is the photonic switch. The Self Electro-optic Effect Devices (or SEEDs) are activated by the arrival of a photon of light, which generates a voltage that in turn changes the light transmission characteristics of the SEED. Current technology can manufacture a SEED of 2,500 alternating layers of gallium arsenide and gallium aluminium arsenide with supporting circuitry all within a thickness of six-thousandth of a millimetre.[9] Advances using this type of device are particularly promising for the parallel processing of data, which can enter from the top of the chip and emerge at the bottom, rather than the more conventional sequential processing systems.

While there is still room for development through the utilization of electronic switching processes, the capacity of the human brain suggests that the most productive long-term research will be in the field of biochemical computers. The brain is still poorly understood but appears to be able to cram at least 10^{14} junctions into a box the size of the skull. The processing system is parallel, redundant and self-manufacturing. It would be surprising if the chemical and electrical connections of the brain had no lessons to offer to the computer scientist. Research is already well under way into electronic simulations of the brain's neural network.[10] Such systems are already able to carry out collective decision computing.

Computers of whatever power remain useless boxes until they are instructed how to process information. The earliest machines were wired up so that the operations required were carried out in the necessary order. The development of instructions as part of the input data allowed the development of modern computers. Originally these instructions had to be laboriously written to tell the computer in detail each step required. Thus, if numbers were to be added they would have to be converted into the binary system, stored at specified locations in the computer memory, brought into the central processing unit to be added one by one, and the result sent to another memory location. To ease this task, operations which were used repeatedly were stored for quick access, and the computer could translate a single mnemonic into the necessary sequence of instructions. Different applications called on different routines and so a range of computer languages has developed. The problem of the development has been to make it as easy as possible to give the computer instructions, while at the same time making them both correct and unambiguous. Machine-dependent languages are different for every processor and are totally specific. However they are difficult to trace errors in, and take a long time to write. General-purpose languages like BASIC are easy for the non-specialist to use but lack rigorous checking systems to ensure that the machine is correctly instructed, and is not standardized between machines. What is required is a language with universal application, which is standard between the whole range of computing devices, does not use up the machine's processing capability in translating the instructions, has the ability to detect errors and allows programs to be easily understood and modified.

The advantages of such work on standardization has led to the adoption of ADA by the US armed forces as their preferred language. However languages currently require specialist training for the giving of instructions to computers. The tendency has been to make the job of the operator as easy as possible. As computing power has increased, it has been possible to make available capacity for the computer to guide the operator through the instruction process. For the future, the realms of artificial intelligence seem to offer the greatest potential for new languages exploiting the capabilities of the greater computational power.

The definition of artificial intelligence remains a somewhat emotive issue. As the capabilities of computers has expanded, the definition of intelligence has been pushed further and further back, until it appears that it becomes defined as that process of reasoning which is beyond the capability of current machines. The first computers were configured for a particular process. The development of programming languages allowed machines to be used for many applications through different programs. More recently the operator has been able to instruct the machine more generally about problems, and it has generated the program to cover the task. Programs which allow a machine to learn by experience and modify the program accordingly are already in current usage. In the same way computers can operate on incomplete data and make a best guess. The increases in computer power and speed allow these abilities to be improved, and hence the machine becomes more intelligent. The design of the program is also a vital part of this process. Brute force analysis of problems limits the size of the problem that can be solved. If chess-playing computers attempted to examine every possible move and countermove they would have to consider of the order of 10^{120} possibilities. Successful chess players, both human and computer, reduce the number of possibilities they examine by looking at 'promising' options. The rules which guide the computer to select a manageable number of options determine the intelligence of its game. If those rules can be modified by experience by the computer then it can improve its performance further. Such systems already exist, and the development of techniques to improve intelligence is a major area for further research.[11]

Having reviewed briefly the developments and possibilities of computer science, what are the implications for the military? Already the computer is an essential component of every aspect of war. From the digital clock in the terrorist bomb to the supercomputer simulating the nuclear explosion in a new warhead, modern warfare depends on computer devices. For the gathering of intelligence, computers can assess information, compare multiple sources, analyse the information and present it in time for it to be of use. Computer guidance of weapon systems allows navigation systems to work to accuracy measured in centimetres over ranges quantified in thousands of kilometres. No longer is accuracy a function of range. In communication systems, computers have brought true security through encryption. In military aircraft, computer control allows designs that are inherently unstable and thus offer great agility in combat. Artillery computers can control army firepower. At sea, the ship's captain can fight from deep within his vessel using computer-generated information from all his sensors. Under the sea, the strategic submarine depends on computers to run the nuclear power system, and each missile must be linked into the navigational computer. When the missile is fired the on-board computer will control its flight-path to strike its target. In the cruise missile, the computer is able to compare the ground over which the missile is flying with its expected contours, and update the navigational information accordingly. The list could go on endlessly. There is no doubt that computers are important to military technology. The question for the future is what areas of research in this field will have the greatest potential to improve military capability, and what vulnerabilities result from the universal application of computers?

The advent of more powerful systems will be particularly important in the acquisition, analysis and dissemination of timely information. Today the cycle time for reconnaissance, analysis, mission-tasking and execution is measured in hours, whether one considers space-based sensor systems, aircraft or even foot patrols. The ability to data-link various sensor systems through a powerful computer, and retransmit the analysed information to the firepower system in a timely way is one of the most urgent requirements. Such technology, while complex, is designed to ease the decision-making problem of the soldier. But reliance on such systems can lead to unquestioning reactions, as the shooting down of a civil airliner by the American warship *Vincennes* showed in 1988.[12] Nevertheless, the infantryman holding a portable air defence missile does not wish to know the speed, temperature, altitude, radar shape, exhaust characteristics or heading of the aircraft in his sight. He does not need to know the larger airspace management picture, and how his target fits into it. The computer can look at all the evidence from many sources and determine the probability of the target being an enemy aircraft. For the soldier in the field, his display need be no more than a green or red light to indicate friend or foe. Computer power and artificial intelligence have much to offer in this area.[13]

Weapons have become more accurate and effective as sensor systems have become small enough to include in the weapon. As the computer power that can be included in a missile increases, so the weapon needs to depend less on the human operator. It is sometimes suggested that this offers the prospect of the automated battlefield. At its most dramatic, this automation is assumed in the nuclear deterrence posture of launch on warning. Concerns over the possibility of losing retaliatory capability to a pre-emptive strategic attack has led to the suggestion that missiles could be launched when a massive attack was detected, but before the enemy missiles arrived at their targets. The short time of flight of ballistic missiles means that such a system would require computer analysis of the sensor data indicating a massive enemy launch of offensive missiles. If the analysis confirmed such an attack then the computer would activate the retaliatory strike. Such a 'Doomsday Machine' is unlikely to find favour, whatever the improvements in sensor technology, computer power and machine reliability. But is it possible that an analogous automatic system could be used on the conventional battlefield? One can conceive of an intelligent reconnaisance drone searching an area for enemy tanks, activating a surface-to-surface missile with multiple terminally-guided munitions, and hence destroying the tanks. The drone would carry out the post-attack analysis and decide whether further attack was necessary. The possibilities of such systems would depend crucially on the computer's ability to recognize decoy schemes and counter them. The predictability of the system which lacks human intervention is currently a great weakness. Nevertheless, this type of warfare may become possible, and research will certainly be important.

Moving from the use of computers for the tactical battle to their application at the strategic and policy level, war games on computers are already important for both planning and training. If the most massive computers can model the workings of the earth's atmosphere, will they not also be able to predict the right strategy and tactics to win wars? Here the prospects seem less certain. The difficulties of modelling human qualities, political will, public opinion and the many subjective factors which affect the outcome of a conflict, make the prospects for computer prediction rather less likely than accurate economic forecasting. As a training aid in war, from the individual simulator for a soldier operating an anti-tank missile, through the air-to-air combat simulator, to the full command and control war simulator, increasing computing power is important. Simulation can also be used to provide insights into physical processes, which cannot be tested in the real world: space weapons, nuclear reactions and catastrophic destructive processes.[14]

The very usefulness of the computer brings with it the penalty of dependence. The fineness of the component-integrated circuits make them sensitive to their environment. In particular excess voltages can destroy the circuitry efficiently. Of particular concern is the electro-magnetic pulse (EMP) which accompanies any nuclear explosion. Military electronics are now routinely, though at considerable expense, protected against expected EMP levels. Administrative systems and civilian computers are not given such protection. Yet the destruction of such systems would have a crucial effect on how well a modern nation could fight. The military machine is moving towards a total dependence on the availability of its computer systems. This suggests that a productive line of research may be in anti-computer weapons. It may be the directed energy weapon will prove to have a unique use after all. In particular, the use of high energy radio frequency weapons could prove to be a potent counter to systems dependent on micro-electronics. Alternatively the targeting by conventional weapons of computer centres may prove to be a cheaper, yet effective, tactic.

The final question to be considered is the division of effort in computer research. The military needs have been important in the history of computer development so far. Commercial exploitation has followed and reduced unit costs. Pure research in mathematics, physics, biochemistry and computer science is likely to produce useful progress with applications to the military. There will, however, remain the specialized needs of the military fields, which will require specific defence research and development. Perhaps the area to give the greatest return will be the exploitation of the enemy's reliance on computers.

CHAPTER 7

Nuclear Physics

OF ALL the fields of modern science, nuclear physics is unarguably the one which has provided the ultimate weapon so far. As a branch of theoretical physics it has made great strides since the first development of atomic weapons. To what extent have these subsequent discoveries had a military utility, and what further applications are in prospect for the future?

The story of the development of the atomic bomb is well known, the first experiments in radioactive decay taking place at the end of the last century. Einstein's theoretical prediction that mass and energy were equivalent, and that the transformation of mass into energy would release vast amounts of energy, made the atom bomb a theoretical possibility. Atomic theory brought new insights into the nature of the atom and developed, hand-in-hand with quantum theory, to predict atomic behaviour. By 1933 enough pieces of the jigsaw were there for one scientist to predict that 'a chain reaction might be set up if an element could be found that would emit two neutrons when it swallows one neutron'.[1] The discovery that uranium atoms did just this came in 1939, and from then on it was as much a problem of engineering as of physics to produce the fission bomb.

Much greater mass change, and hence energy change, was theoretically possible through the fusion of lighter elements into heavier ones than through the fission of heavy to light. The difficulty in fusing atoms together was that very high temperatures were necessary to trigger the process. This was the mechanism which kept the stars in the sky shining for millennia. The development of the thermonuclear bomb in the early 1950s demonstrated that fusion was achievable by using a fission weapon to provide the detonator. This meant that the yield of any nuclear weapon could be increased virtually without limit. Less obvious at the time, but of greater significance subsequently, has been the ability to make nuclear weapons smaller in size and of lower yield. The nuclear artillery shell, the missile warhead and the multiple warhead all became possible.

There is no doubt that the military needs pushed forward nuclear physics in the early days. The construction of early nuclear power stations stemmed from the need to produce fissile material. Since then the fields of theoretical nuclear physics have overlapped more and more with those of high energy physics which were considered in Chapter 5. Nevertheless nuclear tests continue, and for a brief period in the 1970s the prospect of an enhanced radiation weapon (the neutron bomb) excited popular interest. Nuclear physicists had not been idle in the intervening years. The destructive power of nuclear weapons depends on the combination of a number of different effects. Typically the energy released by a fission type explosion is made up of 50 per cent blast, 35 per cent thermal radiation, 5 per cent prompt radiation and 10 per cent residual radiation. If a pure fusion weapon were possible then the proportions might be 20 per cent blast and thermal, with the major 80 per cent of energy being released as prompt radiation, and very little residual radiation. However, the pure fusion weapon is not as yet possible, and developments aimed at altering the balance between the fission trigger and the fusion element of the bomb have only modified the radiation element by a small margin. The enhanced radiation 8-inch artillery shell is claimed to produce only 10 per cent enhancement in prompt radiation.[2] The advantages of a weapon which leaves less residual radiation, and has a more precise blast effect, is to make its use appear more credible to an enemy. This is particularly necessary in the case of short-range weapons where the effects on friendly forces are critical. Yet the difference between the enhanced radiation weapon and the normal atomic shell is only at the margins. Indeed this appears to be the difficulty in many of the possible improvements in nuclear capabilities. The warheads can now be made as small as necessary, with whatever yield is required, and the development of different nuclear mechanisms seems to offer little advantage. There was a time when the atomic bullet seemed a logical development of the smaller and smaller atomic devices but now the strategic realities of the command and control of nuclear weapons makes this a route of little interest.

The enhanced radiation weapon is seen by some to offer a significant improvement in nuclear deterrent capability. The prompt radiation would disable troops even in tanks, without the penalty of collateral damage and long-term radiation. One route to achieve this would be through a pure fusion weapon. Current thermonuclear weapons gain their energy from lithium deuteride producing tritium after irradiation by the neutrons from the uranium or plutonium fission reaction; and subsequent fusing of the tritium isotope of hydrogen into heavier elements. The energy in the fission bomb provides the temperatures and pressures necessary for sufficient time to cause the fusion process, which then releases the high energy associated with thermonuclear devices. Much development work is in progress in the civil sector towards taming the fusion process. As considerably more energy is released in the fusion of atoms than is necessary to initiate the process, there appears to be the prospect of limitless cheap power. While success in this field would have very significant implications for power generation (see Chapter 5), it is unlikely to affect nuclear weapon design. The two fields, while overlapping, have different objectives: the military seeks instantaneous fusion power; the civil seeks controlled prolonged fusion power. Currently one area might serve both: laser-initiated fusion. The concentration in energy possible with high power lasers seems to offer the prospect of containing sufficient energy to initiate fusion. The successful development of a civil power generator based on such a device might well offer possibilities for a pure fusion weapon. The other routes being followed by civil researchers follow the large-scale engineering inappropriate to weapon development.

While a pure fusion weapon could offer advantages in cost, size, lack of residual radiation and a move away from dependence on uranium and plutonium, there are a number of areas for research into improvements in the fission and fission-fusion weapons of today. The enhanced radiation weapon has demonstrated that it is possible to optimize the weapon for a particular form of damage (although the other forms of damage are not eliminated). All nuclear weapons have similar effects.[3] The balance of damage caused by heat, blast and radiation can be altered by changing the yield or by altering the height of the detonation between a ground burst and a height at which the fireball no longer touches the ground. Yet in every case the energy is radiated out as an expanding sphere until it meets resistance. A bullet is highly directional. Anti-tank shells have shaped charges to penetrate in the direction which will give most lethality to a tank. Mines are arranged to fire their charges up into the vulnerable parts of vehicles. Yet nuclear weapons remain like the cartoon anarchist's bomb: equally destructive in all directions. This suggests that energy is wasted and collateral damage is more difficult to control. One can visualize targets in which an asymmetry of nuclear effect would be advantageous. A nuclear weapon designed to destroy enemy missile silos would be improved if the nuclear effects could be channelled forward in a cylinder with dimensions related to the accuracy of delivery. A battlefield nuclear weapon would be improved if all its effects could be concentrated in the enemy's direction without danger to friendly forces. There seems no reason why development of such asymmetries in nuclear effects could not be developed along the lines of the shaped charges of conventional explosives. The question is whether the advantages derived are sufficient to outweigh the costs of development.

The next area to consider for nuclear weapon development is whether the primary and secondary effects of a nuclear explosion are amenable to change, and if so what advantages can be gained. Looking at the possibilities for the future, one writer[4] has identified fifteen different areas where selective enhancement of nuclear effects could improve capabilities. By changing the average molecular weight of the materials in the weapon, the surface area and the energy distribution the device could be optimized for the production of X-rays. Such a weapon detonated in space could be used to damage ballistic missiles during their exo-atmospheric phase and against satellites. Work has also been in progress on the X-ray laser which would be excited by the nuclear explosion. This would allow much greater concentration of X-ray energy flux, assuming that it could be directed against the target in space. X-rays are absorbed by the atmosphere, although generating an Electromagnetic Pulse (EMP) in the process. This EMP can effect electronic devices and radio communications. The weapon might instead be optimized for gamma ray, microwave, infra-red, radio frequency or visible light emission. Such devices exploded in space or in the atmosphere will have different characteristics. If the radiation is focused or directed, it can be more damaging but requires accurate control. The EMP effect can be optimized in a number of ways. The type of fall-out could be tailored to the required effect. The bomb debris could be transformed from the minor part it currently plays into a directed projectile. Were such a development possible, a nuclear projectile (one in which the motive force is provided by a nuclear explosion) might be able to shoot down vehicles in space and the upper atmosphere.

There are, therefore, in prospect a large number of avenues for the development of nuclear weapons, and most would require exclusively military funding. Given the political realities of the use of nuclear weapons, there seems little point in devoting great resources to fields where, whatever the military potential, the weapons could not be used. Currently a number of nuclear systems exist in order to complicate enemy planning. While battlefield weapons would be unlikely to be used at an early stage of a conflict in Europe, they force ground forces to deploy in a disadvantageous manner. It could be that the possibility of concentrated EMP-generating devices would also complicate enemy assumptions on assessments of success of electronic systems. Nuclear devices which were detonated on home territory might appear more credible for early use. Thus an underground nuclear device which fired directed radiation or projectiles from friendly territory could be a productive area for development. This might well be a productive area for terminal defence against both conventional and nuclear ballistic missiles. The use of a nuclear device on home territory would not be the signal for the start of a nuclear exchange between protagonists. There are, however, a number of political difficulties with a concept which requires the detonation of nuclear weapons on home territory in time of conflict. Indeed, the greater public awareness after the Chernobyl disaster of the widespread contamination possible from nuclear sources makes such developments unattractive.

In any analysis of the most productive areas for research in military uses of nuclear physics, the political dimension must be considered. The Partial Test Ban Treaty of 1963 inhibits considerably the development of weapons whose interaction with the atmosphere is of a crucial importance. The Outer Space Treaty of 1967 has a similar effect on those nuclear weapons which capitalize on positioning beyond the atmosphere. Nevertheless computer modelling and underground nuclear tests can produce sufficient data for some novel nuclear weapon development. Nuclear weapons can be improved in ways exactly analogous to conventional weapons. They can be delivered with greater accuracy over greater ranges in shorter response times: the technologies necessary are all non-nuclear. What nuclear physics can provide is a weapon which is optimized for a particular target, and improvements in ease of production, cost and maintenance of the weapons. Within the area of target optimization, it is likely that the most productive area for research is generating electromagnetic energy for offensive purposes. As dependence on electrical and electronic systems increases, the vulnerability to enemy-induced failures of these systems also increases. The EMP associated with a nuclear explosion is already a cause of considerable concern, and great expenditure is incurred in taking protective measures to reduce the effect. This effect is greatest in exo-atmospheric or high altitude explosions. There are two different EMP generators. The plasma passing through the earth's magnetic field causes a broad band surge of electromagnetic radiation. In addition the ionizing of the atmosphere by gamma and X-rays produces a current from the flow of electrons, which in turn produces electromagnetic radiation. It is, however, conceivable that a weapon could be designed to produce much more of its energy as a narrower band of electromagnetic radiation. If the wavelength is selected so that propagation in the atmosphere is unimpeded, then protection becomes much more difficult and the yield of weapons can be much reduced for a given damage level. Microwave radiation in the centimetre wavelength band seems particularly well suited to this role. Even a relatively small proportion of a nuclear explosion that could be channelled into microwave radiation could wreak havoc on computer systems, microprocessor control systems, power sources, communication systems and all things electrical. This would have considerable implications for command and control arrangements.

The final area where nuclear physics may have significant implications for nuclear weapons is in the manufacturing processes. The relatively slow proliferation of nuclear states has, to a considerable extent, been a function of the difficulties in producing weapon grade nuclear material, and then of the engineering problems in producing a reliable weapon. The processing to separate different isotopes of uranium has been a complex and expensive undertaking involving a highly specialized engineering and chemical facilities. Research into simpler methods for normal industrial use will inevitably make the technology available to a wider number of nations. In addition the civil research into fusion power previously discussed may lead to simpler forms of nuclear weapon, which can be more easily manufactured. Such developments might have significant implications for the availability of nuclear weapons.

Turning away from the weapons aspects of nuclear physics, there are other influences which this branch of research can have on security interests. Nuclear power has had a somewhat chequered career in the civil sector, and the problems of safety and waste-disposal continue to cause disquiet, and hence slow down the rate of development. On the military side the cost and constraints of nuclear power systems has restricted their use to where the operational need is over-riding, as in nuclear submarines, or where the power required can be produced economically, as in aircraft carriers. The developments in controlled fusion power already discussed may change the balance of advantage both in the civil and military sectors. This however is in the longer term, and currently the size of potential fusion power generators gives little hope for them being integrated into mobile systems.[5] In any event, the research being undertaken in the civil sector will allow the military possibilities to be anticipated.

One aspect of nuclear power which does have strategic implications is the availability of civil nuclear power stations as targets. The destruction of such a facility by conventional weapons would allow an enemy to generate many of the effects of a nuclear strike without using nuclear weapons. The long-term and widespread effects of the fire at the Chernobyl plant in 1986 indicated what a major disaster could be caused by a damaged nuclear power station. Two connected areas of research can thus be useful: one offensive and one defensive. Custom-made conventional weapons designed to cause a nuclear power plant to run out of control would be complex, and would depend on the design of the various safety features in the target. The destruction of the protective containment vessel would stop power production and cause local contamination. For a Chernobyl-scale effect, the safety features must be countered. This then leads to consideration of defences against such weapon developments by a potential enemy. There are passive measures such as the siting of power stations in isolated locations, and taking heed of the prevailing winds. These are sensible precautions in any event. What is also necessary at the design stage of any nuclear power station is consideration of the redundancy and hardening of all safety features against a conventional weapon attack. In this regard over-insurance is to be encouraged, as modifications at a later stage will be very difficult. The use of nuclear power stations as weapons which bridge the nuclear threshold may have received insufficient attention in the past.

CHAPTER 8

Space Technology

IT IS not quite honest to look at space technology as a separate area for research. It is made up of a multitude of different scientific disciplines. From the chemistry of rocket propellant, through the mathematics of orbital calculations to the psychology of isolation in zero gravity conditions, no area of modern science is left unrepresented. It is, however, valid to consider it as a collection of new technologies directed towards the common exploitation of the vast region of the universe beyond our atmosphere. The first satellite placed in orbit was *Sputnik 1* in October 1957. The implications for the strategic balance at the time were profound. Yet in the thirty years that have followed, the military exploitation of space has been surprisingly limited.[1]

The first area of intensive research is in the space vehicle provision. Single-shot ballistic rockets have assumed a vital role in nuclear delivery and satellite emplacement, and show prospects for conventional warfare. In this respect civil and military needs have run in parallel as the demands for communications satellites for civil use have increased. That said, the military use has driven the technology, and is likely to continue doing so. The high cost of expendable space systems led to the development of the space shuttle by the United States. However, experience of the shuttle in use has not yet given convincing proof that launch costs have been reduced. The major lesson of the first three decades in space is that the costs of breaking free from the earth's gravity remain very high. If the physical law of conservation of energy is to remain valid, there is little prospect of reducing this high cost of space operations. It is, therefore, important that whatever is done in space is provided at minimum weight, and the development of microprocessor technology has made this possible. Research will continue into rocket propulsion and vehicle design, but a major breakthrough in reduction in launch costs from the earth's surface to orbit is unlikely.

Research is actively under way on the development of hybrid aircraft/rockets which can use conventional aircraft techniques to reach the upper atmosphere, whence they can launch into low earth orbit. While these developments may improve the reliability of reusable space vehicles, they are unlikely to change the payload costs much. The highest that conventional aircraft operate is at around twenty miles, and at this distance from the earth the gravitational potential is little less than at the surface.

If the costs of raising objects from ground level to orbit are to remain high, the effectiveness of what is put into orbit must be an area for productive research. While the prospects of weapons in space attracts much topical interest, all man-made devices in space today are either civil, military but non-offensive, or inert. Anti-satellite weapons have been tested, and will be considered later in this Chapter. Other space-based weapon systems remain in the research laboratory. Space today is home to a range of military satellites whose roles are reconnaissance, communications, navigation, meteorology and geodetic survey.

Reconnaissance satellites exploit a wide range of the electromagnetic spectrum. Electronic intelligence can be gathered from radio and radar signals. Early warning of missile launch is gained from infra-red sensors observing the missile exhaust. The visible and near visible region can provide traditional strategic and tactical reconnaissance information. The areas for productive research to improve military capability revolve around the normal reconnaissance cycle. In this the time between initiating the task and receiving the processed information must be as short as possible, the quality of the information must be as good as possible, and the interpretation of the data must be as accurate as possible.

The propagation characteristics of particular wavelengths of electromagnetic radiation in the atmosphere make satellite reconnaissance less than totally reliable. They can only complement an overall intelligence picture obtained from aircraft and human sources. Nevertheless improvements in sensors will improve sensitivity and discrimination. More active scanning may offer improved results. Radar or laser emitters from the satellite could illuminate specific targets. One particular area where successful research could have a dramatic effect on strategic stability is in the detection of submarines under the ocean. Techniques being explored include high-power lasers, magnetic anomaly detection, small temperature anomaly detection, radar, and sea surface movement.[2] None of these seem to offer the solution to making the oceans transparent, but they aid submarine detection.

Reducing the time taken for the reconnaissance cycle is also amenable to novel techniques. While some satellites can be placed in geosynchronous orbit to monitor a particular area, their distance from the surface reduces definition. If they are placed in low orbit to improve quality, they cannot hold station over one area, and only a part of their orbit will be useful. This can be compensated for by the use of a number of satellites which weave a pattern of orbits to ensure the required level of coverage of the target. This multiplies the cost. For particular operations it may be worth while launching a reconnaissance satellite into a predetermined orbit for the one mission: an expensive option. While such satellites have the ability to move orbit from their own power sources, such provision is finite and once the fuel is exhausted they will soon decay and burn up. It is possible to envisage drone satellites being launched from a space station for particular missions, and recovered at the end of the task for refuel. It is not obvious that the benefits would outweigh the costs, unless the space station were justified on other grounds.

The utility of a space station is something which is worth examining separately. Many future projections of military use of space start from the assumption that such a platform will be available. A space station is generally assumed to be a continously manned orbiting structure, which allowed a range of space tasks to be carried out, with regular replenishment from Earth. Without specifying the nature of the platform, costs are inevitably speculative. Van Allen has suggested a figure of $30 billion (1984 dollars) for the NASA-proposed development from 1993.[3] The Soviet Union has been at the forefront of research into prolonged manned spaceflight and is operating a rudimentary manned space station with docking facilities. The real question is whether the presence of men is of such vital importance that it outweighs the cost of the associated support systems. Whether systems are launched from Earth, or assembled in orbit on a space station, they still require the same overall expenditure of energy to put them into orbit. A space station requires the additional energy costs of raising its own support service elements into orbit. The costs benefits, as opposed to the prestige benefits, are not obvious and the balance of cost advantage between manned and unmanned space systems shows little sign of changing in the future.

The second class of satellites to be considered are those used for communications. Here military and civilian development has gone in parallel. Indeed to the man in the street, communication satellites have been the prime area of progress through the exploitation of space. Worldwide telephone, television and data transmission are now ordinary aspects of modern life. Development work continues in order to provide more powerful television relays from orbit to cover larger areas of the world. In the military sphere, satellites have brought into reality the ability to communicate securely over any distance with total reliability. The vagaries of the ionosphere, which used to make HF communications such a black art, have been replaced by a worldwide communication capability as clear and dependable as line-of-sight VHF radio.[4]

Such communications can transform military effectiveness, but also carry penalties. The ease with which command and control can be exercised from the highest to the lowest formation through satellite-based communications makes the military ever more dependent on them. The old back-up methods of HF radio, landline and runner become even less reliable through lack of use. Yet in a future war, satellite communications could be a very productive area for offensive action. The effect of EMP has already been discussed, and more selective anti-satellite measures will be considered later. Nevertheless, research in both civil and military sectors will lead to more powerful satellite relay facilities which will reduce the size of the communication equipment required on the ground.

Satellite navigation systems have been in operation since 1960. They provided information for updating inertial navigation systems on strategic missiles. The systems currently under development (GLONASS in the Soviet Union, and NAVSTAR GPS in the United States) will offer highly accurate worldwide three-dimensional position-fixing.[5] This will give benefits in both the civil and military fields. Aircraft will be able to operate in greater safety, or to much less constraining operating limitations. When combined with the satellite communications network, the commander will be able to have an accurate picture of the disposition of his forces at all times. Combine that information with the processed data from reconnaissance systems, and some of the 'fog of war' is dispersed. A real change in the nature of command of the battle becomes possible if the commander is to sit back in a secure area running the tactical situation from a combined display of friendly and enemy forces. Again this apparent advance carries the danger of reliance on vulnerable satellite systems.

Satellites for meteorology and geodetic survey also have military implications. They can provide data for strategic missiles, or tactical weather information for the battlefield commander. The quantity of data which can be obtained, when coupled to the increasingly powerful computers, offers more accurate, detailed and longer term forecasting. The availability of either type of satellite in war is unlikely to be critical.

The area of space technology which offers most profit for investigation is that of anti-satellite (ASAT) warfare. As discussed above, the new capabilities brought by satellite systems are making armed forces increasingly dependent and hence vulnerable. A productive area for research is to seek ways to destroy satellites. Such offensive systems may be ground-based, air-launched or space-based. ASAT may be widespread in effect, localized or selective against particular systems.

Systems under development include an ASAT missile launched by a high-flying aircraft (US), and a manoeuvrable exploding satellite (USSR). Possible developments include the use of appropriate frequency laser damage weapons to blind reconnaissance systems. The exploding satellite could be developed into a space mine system, or a missile could expel shrapnel to cause mechanical damage. Should a manned space station be built, then selective ASAT weapons could be used. Directed energy and kinetic energy kill mechanism would both be useful techniques in space.

The other part of the ASAT question is development of defensive measures. This is a much more difficult problem. Blacking out sensors under attack is one avenue. Mobility and offensive firepower on otherwise passive satellites may be another. Indeed the future of ASAT warfare begins to sound like the development of air warfare. Its major difference is in the cost of such systems. It may be that ultimately the only defence against pre-emptive satellite destruction is to ensure that military forces do not become totally dependent on the systems. Certainly the advantage of control of space is such that it could be war winning. It appears therefore that ASAT research is a major requirement for defence funding. Some place their hopes in arms control negotiations outlawing such research or deployment. The argument is that it is in the interests of both of the superpowers to be able to have assured use of satellite systems for strategic reconnaissance and communication. The world is a safer place when both know that the other can detect and react to a surprise attack; and hence no such attack takes place. The fallacy in this argument is that such a treaty is practically unenforceable. The technologies have many applications and can be rapidly adapted for ASAT work.[6] It is therefore important that both realize that the destruction of one state's satellites by the other will earn retribution in kind. This means that ASAT research is a vital area.

The use of weapons in space for the limited purpose of denying an enemy the use of his satellite systems brings us to the wider consideration of war in space. Since 1983, when President Reagan first looked to scientists to provide protection against strategic nuclear weapons, the Strategic Defence Initiative (SDI) has kept war in space a topical issue. The research undertaken since seeks to provide a system which can destroy nuclear ballistic missiles in flight. Research has been directed towards providing a layered system. In this, missiles would be attacked during their initial launch period when the hot exhaust gases of the rocket motor, and the relatively slower speeds, make them easier targets. During this period response times must be very short (the boost phase lasts only 2–5 minutes). Those that got through this defence would then be attacked during the ballistic mid-course period when the independent warheads separate from the missile. Here there are problems with acquisition, decoys and kill assessment. Finally those missiles penetrating the second layer would have to be destroyed by a final defensive screen designed to destroy warheads re-entering the atmosphere.

The strategic arguments over the utility of such a defensive system continue to rage.[7] While the technical arguments about kinetic energy and directed energy weapon feasibility will take years to answer, all agree on the high cost of all systems involved. Figures approaching $1,000 billion are suggested as an order of magnitude for deploying a space-based defensive system. The system must have target surveillance and acquisition systems, discrimination against decoys, pointing and tracking systems, kill assessment capability, appropriate weapons, and an overall command and control arrangement. All these require new developments in technology, and can ultimately only provide a limited defence against nuclear weapons. Assuming the highly unlikely possibility that a space-based defensive system worked first time (no real test would ever be possible) and eliminated most ballistic missiles, that would still leave the prospect of nuclear attack by cruise missiles, aircraft and man-carried systems.

It seems, therefore, that a large amount of research resources are likely to be absorbed in SDI work which, even if successful, will not offer the possibility of either military advantage or an improvement in strategic stability. The argument is often advanced that the spin-off for other military research from such a large project is a major consideration. Certainly there will be considerable enhancements to more mundane weapon systems as a result. This cannot be a justification: the improvements would be much greater if the resources were directed towards the particular problem area. If research and development for ballistic missile defence is to absorb so much effort, it must be because of its own merits. Those seem arguable at present, whereas the cost is not.

Given that nations may nevertheless continue development of space-based defensive systems, research to counter the systems will remain important. Fortunately the counter systems are, by and large, both cheaper and less complex. Defence against directed-energy weapons through materials technology will pay dividends. The reduction of boost phase time for missiles and the improvement of decoy systems will also prove fruitful. However the solution to a partially capable missile defence system may be simply to increase the number of offensive missiles. While this does little to help arms control, it will be an appealing answer to states in the future.

Moving from defensive to offensive weapons in space, the field is wide open. It is argued that some of the SDI technologies could have offensive possibilities. In the past, schemes for orbiting nuclear weapons were considered. Fortunately common sense has prevailed. While they might offer slightly shorter response times to anywhere on the planet, they would be destabilizing and also potentially hazardous both on launch and recovery. The exotic directed energy weapons designed for counter-missile use might have applications against aircraft or cruise missiles. The atmosphere provides considerable protection, and the countermeasures could do much to reduce effectiveness. Conventional missiles could be fired from space-based launchers; but the energy bill to put them in orbit must still be paid, and the advantages are difficult to see.

One kinetic energy system which is under development is the electromagnetic rail gun. In this a small projectile is accelerated to speeds of 5–25km/sec. The power requirements for such a system are likely to be prohibitive, but it is possible to envisage it having a greater application than just anti-missile operations in space. If the acceleration takes place from orbit, speed reduction when it is fired into the atmosphere will be minimal. The problem then becomes one of burn-up. As a system against high-flying aircraft it may have application, but again at a cost which is likely to be prohibitive.

Nowhere more than in space technology does the excitement and glamour of research override the mundane considerations of military cost effectiveness. The history of the space age carries all the necessary warnings: progress has been slow and costly. Following the US space shuttle disaster, and a series of unmanned launcher failures, the US has found it difficult even to keep up with its routine satellite launch requirements. Grandiose schemes in space all have to answer the question of the energy costs in placing a given mass into orbit. High power weapons call for higher energy cost. In only one area does it appear that research and development will have significant security implications and that is ASAT. The ability to destroy satellites may become crucial, particularly if the enemy has such a capability.

CHAPTER 9

Chemistry

CHEMISTRY is a branch of science which can all too readily be discounted as potentially fruitful for military applications. While we will consider chemical weapons in the narrow sense in this Chapter, they represent only one application of chemicals to war. The great achievement of the early chemists was the production of gunpowder, and it is in the field of explosives that they may have much to offer still. As with so many aspects of modern military technology, the new weapons draw on many disciplines. Chemical reactions can provide power in the form of explosive release of energy, or as a controlled propulsive force. Chemicals can kill through direct effects on different vital functions of human beings, and they can also provide the protection against such weapons. They can provide healing drugs to heal casualties rapidly, or disabling drugs to affect the will of a soldier to fight. Chemicals can be used to attack indirectly through the food chain, or can provide extra resources through fertilizers and pest control. In sum, chemistry is used offensively and defensively and, as with so much of modern science, the products of civilian research play an important role in the security of a nation.

In modern strategic jargon, chemical warfare refers only to the use of chemical substances which kill or disable living organisms. While chemical weapons may be dropped on buildings or equipment or dispersed over territory, it is done to deny access by vulnerable men. Agents are characterized by five qualities: Stability, Potency, Persistence, Delay Time and Cost of Production.[1] Stability is a measure of how well a particular chemical agent retains its potency. Technical developments have worked towards producing stable agents which can be more easily stored and handled, while at the same time remaining effective for many years. The recent production of binary nerve agents in the United States has greatly enhanced the stability factor of chemical agents. Potency reflects the amount of agent necessary to produce the desired effect. Development work directed towards increasing potency allows either a wider area to be covered, or greater range with reduced warhead payload. Some agents disperse and lose their effectiveness in a relatively short-time (often depending on

77

wind); others can remain effective for days. The tactical situation will determine whether a persistent or non-persistent agent is preferable. The delay time is a measure of the time taken between contact with an agent and the onset of the required effect. It will normally be advantageous to minimize the delay time. Finally the cost of production of any chemical agents is important as large quantities are required for effective operations and technology can be directed towards minimizing unit costs.

The current range of available chemical weapons attack the target's vital systems in different ways. Blister agents causing burns and skin blisters date from mustard gas in World War I. Lethal concentrations are difficult to achieve, and protection is relatively easy. Blood gases, like Hydrogen Cyanide, interfere with cell respiration. Protection can be achieved through the use of gas masks, but it is possible rapidly to saturate the breathing filter with such agents. Lung irritants, such as Phosgene, attack the respiratory system and, again, gas masks provide protection. Nerve agents affect the body's ability to control muscle action, and lead to death through respiratory failure. Some, such as Sarin, must be inhaled, while the V agents can be absorbed through the skin. They are rapid in effect and can be either non-persistent or much longer lasting low volatile substances. Protection can only be achieved by whole body and gas mask coverage.

There are occasions when chemicals which incapacitate rather than kill are more appropriate. This is certainly the case with riot control agents, and also in certain counter-terrorist operations. To incapacitate an individual, it is possible to attack either the body or the mind with chemicals. The widely used phosgene-oxime (CX gas) incapacitates by causing severe nose and eye irritation. The drug LSD has been suggested as a psycho-chemical agent which would incapacitate by producing hallucinations. However as predictability of effect is an important aspect of the use of incapacitating agents, mind-altering drugs have few attractions at present.

In addition to agents lethal and incapacitating to mankind, it is also possible to target other living organisms. Between 1965 and 1971, the US sprayed the South Vietnam jungle with some 10.6m gallons of defoliant chemical known as Agent Orange. While this was done to expose the enemy, the use of such chemicals on both vegetation and livestock to deny food resources is also possible.

Looking to the future of warfare using the full spectrum of chemical agents, a number of avenues for productive research are apparent. On the offensive side rapid acting agents, with precise and predictable consequences, which can be produced easily and safely are the ideal. The chemical characteristics must take into account the available countermeasures. Properly fitted gas masks reduce toxic concentrations in inhaled air by a factor in excess of 100,000.[2] The filter in the mask uses activated charcoal to absorb vapour, and paper to filter particles. Reagents against specific small molecule chemicals, like hydrogen-cyanide, can also be included. Skin protection can be provided either by impermeable material such as rubber, or liquid repellant air-permeable charcoal-lined material. The latter type of covering is much less tiring to work and rest in. Collective protection for forces can be provided in filtered accommodation. The other necessary part of the defensive system is a reliable detector for the presence of chemical agents. Finally, in the event of the chemical being absorbed by the body, it may be possible to administer a chemical antidote. Chemical decontamination is also a requirement if operations are to be continued after an attack by a persistent agent.

Research can offer improvements in the qualities of chemical weapons, the efficiency of protective measures, the success of antidotes and the ease of decontamination. The widespread horror of chemical warfare makes such research controversial in democratic states. Yet the number of nations who may resort to the use of chemical warfare is increasing. As one study into the problem[3] has highlighted, organophosphorus pesticides, which are closely related to nerve agents, are widely used and increasingly produced in the Third World. The production facilities could be used to produce nerve agents, especially as the development of binary weapons has made manufacture that much safer. Even without such an ability, some of the pesticides themselves can act as chemical warfare agents in high concentrations. While comprehensive chemical disarmament is an aim to be welcomed, there is little prospect of universal adherence. The Iran/Iraq war has already shown the impact of chemical weapons. Their use against a civilian town target in 1988 resulted in worldwide publicity. This means that research into chemical warfare will remain an essential part of military technology.

At the lowest end of the spectrum, a riot control agent which disperses a mob without any risk of injury is needed. It may be that research into psycho-chemicals could be productive. It is possible to envisage an agent which could generate short-term amnesia, perhaps an appropriate phobia to cause dispersal of a crowd, or remove all aggression. These are likely to be safer approaches than the agents which produce physical discomfort. Inevitably, the difficulties of predicting concentrations of gas in riot areas make injuries possible through the over-stimulation of body reactions when using those chemicals which produce physical reactions.

In the field of lethal chemical agents, the current range of weapons provides a full spectrum of effectiveness if they are able to penetrate to the targets. Undoubtedly advances can be made in each of the qualities discussed above, but the most productive area for research will be in increasing the penetration of the agents. This has implications for delivery systems and dispersal mechanisms as well as for the chemical composition of the agents. Agents with elements which rapidly saturate filtration systems, or are able to pass through unattenuated, could prove more effective. Perhaps agents which specifically attack the protective materials are possible. Another avenue of approach would be to attempt to deceive detection systems, so that troops had insufficient warning.

All this research runs parallel to the development of improved protection systems. Whatever the outcome of chemical arms control negotiations, it would be wise for nations to retain the technology to protect themselves against this threat. The material for protective clothing must not hamper operations, but must protect against all threats. The filters for gas masks must be both effective and long-lasting. It may be that the development of personal oxygen-generating equipment would offer complete security against inhalation threats. The research in this area must also extend to vehicle and building protection, and will inevitably cover the associated threats from both nuclear and biological weapons.[4]

In the field of countermeasures following chemical contamination, there remains much work to be done. The decontamination of equipment and surfaces of persistent agents is a laborious process. Effective, rapid and cheap decontamination reagents are needed. The antidotes for individuals suffering from chemical exposure are even less satisfactory. For rapid acting agents, there is little time to administer antidotes, which in any event have side effects which incapacitate. The ideal medical countermeasure would be a preventive drug, which would be taken before the chemical attack and would have no side effects. If developed, this panacea drug could alter the balance of advantage in chemical warfare.

Moving away from the narrow definition of chemical warfare to the wider, it is clear that the chemist is a key developer of conventional killing systems. High explosives in munitions and propulsive power from bullets to missiles are all the products of chemical reactions. Improvements in conventional munitions have come from the work of the engineer in designing explosive charges to match specific targets. Nevertheless, the characteristics of the explosives remain a key feature. For a long time weapons have divided into two classes: the target penetrator and the area weapon. In the last century, this would be the difference between the assassin's bullet and the anarchist's bomb. The requirements for each type of weapon system are quite different. For the bullet, shell or missile, accuracy and predictability of propellant are essential. The explosive content can be small, if it is designed to exploit the target's vulnerability. For the area weapon, such as the high explosive bomb, the explosive power for a given weight becomes the important factor. Much work has been done on the development of fuel-air explosives, which can give a large and uniform overpressure over a wide area. The development of explosives with considerable area destructive capability offer attractions to the military commander unable to use tactical nuclear weapons because of escalation considerations.

Development work on chemical propulsive fuels also has far to go. Missile motors have moved from the liquid fuel versions which made them so vulnerable in their slow reaction times. Yet solid-fuel motors require much greater technological expertise if they are to be reliable and predictable. The fuel must not only burn in the expected manner, but must also have a long life without deterioration in performance. At the same time, the more power that can be generated for a given weight of fuel, the greater the warhead that can be delivered over a given distance. All these aspects of propellant design are rich areas for the work of the chemist.

In one other area of propulsion the efficiency of fuel is of critical importance. Military forces depend on fuel oil for nearly all their ships, vehicles and aircraft. While the dire predictions of a world without oil have temporarily been quieted, there is no doubt that oil is a finite natural resource. In any event, the sheer mass of fuel used in war brings with it enormous logistic burdens. Research into fuel technology offers considerable benefits. It may be that an increase in cost of fuel is acceptable if it reduces the capital cost of a particular weapon system. One could envisage an aircraft which required a specific range/payload combination being produced with a simpler design using a more efficient fuel. If fuel could be generated compactly where the army was fighting, its logistic supply problem would be reduced. Rechargeable electric cells offer a clue but remain ludicrously inefficient in power to weight ratios when compared to the internal combustion engine. The development of fuels which allow prolonged operations requires a parallel development of lubricants which can keep mechanical parts operating without attention for longer periods. In both these fields, it is likely that commercial pressures will ensure that research continues which may have military application.

The final area for military interest in the work of the chemist is in pharmacology. The advent of penicillin was as important in warfare as many new weapons. If the aim of a particular weapon is to kill, its effectiveness can be reduced if the rate of survival is increased through medicine. The use of antidotes in chemical warfare has already been discussed. Immunization against biological agents will be considered in Chapter 11. The importance of drugs to promote rapid return of casualties to combat fitness is obvious. Of increasing importance will be drugs to derive maximum effort from troops when required. The advent of 24-hour operations has made the resting of troops even more difficult than in the past. The use of drugs to utilize rest periods fully and to stimulate maximum performance when needed may become the norm. When this extends to drugs which reduce fear or affect the soldier's mind in some other way, a number of difficult moral questions arise. Nevertheless, the possibility of drug-enhanced combat performance is one which cannot be discounted in future conflicts.

The chemist has, therefore, much to offer the military in new technologies. In chemical warfare the research must be virtually exclusively military. Even if the use of such weapons is discounted, there will be a continuing need for research into protective measures. In fuels and propellant technology, commercial considerations are likely to make civil research the most productive path. In healing drugs and techniques, civil medical research will produce applicable techniques. For drugs tailored to enhance performance under the stress of combat, it is likely that a specific research programme would be necessary.

CHAPTER 10

Materials Science

SINCE man discovered how to harden steel, the modification of the molecular structure of materials has had an impact on military effectiveness. Today the nature of materials affects the lethality of weapons, the survivability of troops, the performance of aircraft, the costs of production of new systems and every aspect of every component of defence equipment. The scandal of the aircraft coffee-maker which was designed to a higher *g* tolerance than the aircraft carrying it is a pointer to the pervasiveness of materials technology into every aspect of military hardware.

Looking for greater effectiveness from weapons, we might seek to provide new materials which offer benefits over the old either in capability, ease of manufacture or cost. We must also consider future development in materials which will offer designs not previously possible. The use of carbon-fibre in aircraft to provide greater strength for less weight than conventional materials is now well developed. As is so often the case, there are penalties. The increased strength to weight ratio is bought at the cost of much greater manufacturing difficulties, and hence greater cost. The trade-off in capability against cost is relatively easy to make in the case of aircraft and missiles, where extra mass requires extra power and decreased manoeuvre. In slower surface vehicles the pay-off may not be so clear. Here the productive area for research may be in making manufacturing processes easier and cheaper, and using materials more readily repairable under combat conditions. In this Chapter, we consider the areas where materials technology is important to military effectiveness.

Materials are everywhere. Without them armies would be naked and fighting with bare knuckles. In the past, trial and error sorted out the militarily-useful materials from those of less merit. Some processes, such as the refining of metals, hardening, the making of alloys and the manufacturing developments of the industrial revolution brought great improvements to weapons. Indeed the mechanization of the battlefield was a product of the new material processes of the nineteenth century. However, it is only in this century that the nature of matter has become understood in sufficient detail to tailor materials to requirements. Glass and ceramics, once synonymous with fragility, can today be stronger than steel. Strength, weight, electrical properties, melting points, and all the other characteristics are now being designed, and this has enormous implications for future military equipment.

Every country depends on certain materials for its economic and security wellbeing. The oil crisis of 1973 brought this fact home to the West. There are other less obvious key substances: chromium, manganese, cobalt and platinum. Others are vital, but sources of supply are either so numerous or so secure that they do not worry governments at present. A time may come when quite common materials become scarce, expensive or just unobtainable through exhaustion of supplies or political changes in the supplier countries. Against this possibility nations form strategic stockpiles of particular commodities to help them weather any temporary difficulties. A safer solution is to find an alternative material which can be produced from indigenous resources. Fortunately the impetus for such research is economic and commercial as well as being governed by security considerations. Civil manufacturers do not wish their products to depend on unreliable sources of basic materials, especially if finite resources lead to increasing costs. In some cases smaller quantities of material will be used for a given product. The development of the high-strength low-alloy steels for the motor industry has reduced the weight of the car over the past twenty years significantly. Certain parts are now formed from polymer materials: plastic bumpers and bodywork. The commercial factors at work will be a complex assessment of performance, material costs and manufacturing costs. The relative importance of these factors may, of course, be different for the military. Nevertheless, a complete range of new substitute manufacturing materials is available.

A case of considerable importance is that of aircraft manufacture. A modern high performance aircraft is subject to extreme stresses in every way. Temperatures may vary from –55°C at altitude to supersonic skin temperatures of 500°C, with engine components operating at temperatures over 1,000°C. Ambient pressures vary from atmospheric to near zero, and again jet engines operate at extreme pressures. Manoeuvring may increase component weight by a factor of 10, and such 'g' forces can be applied in very short periods. Engine components also suffer from extreme mechanical loadings, corrosive gases and high vibration levels. It is scarcely surprising, therefore, that the modern and future combat aircraft is crucially dependent on new materials.[1]

While a part of such research is to produce materials which can operate under such extreme conditions, it is important to keep in mind the most crucial criterion: the weight. For a commercial aircraft, reduction in weight reduces operating costs. For a military aircraft, a reduction in weight also brings great benefits. For a given design, a reduction in weight would allow the carriage of more weapon payload, or could increase range for a given fuel load and weapon fit. With the same engine performance, a lower weight aircraft would accelerate faster, climb to altitude more quickly, be better at evading or chasing— depending on its role. A lower weight aircraft could be built to have a smaller radar cross-section to reduce its chance of detection; it could use the spare carrying capability to take self-protective systems; it could be more manoeuvrable. All these measures would improve its chances of survival.

The aerospace industry has been at the forefront of the new materials research and development. Advances have been made in synthesizing new materials and also in the development of composite materials. The material can be designed not just to have great strength but also to grow stronger as the temperature increases.[2] Nickel-based superalloys are strongest at about 850°C, and retain strength to around 1,000°C. This means they can be used in jet engine turbine blade manufacture. Cobalt-based alloys have higher temperature characteristics, but lower overall strength. Where weight is the most critical factor, titanium alloys offer an answer.

Strength can be provided not only by the composition of these alloys, but also by adjusting the crystalline structure of the substance to tailor strength to the role of a particular component. A turbine blade can be given greater strength along its axis of greatest strain through the process of directional solidification. In this the crystals in the alloy are grown in columns by selective heating and cooling. The metal is constructed with unique characteristics for the component. Another advance has been in the process of rapid-solidification technology. Just as the blacksmith would temper his red hot metal by plunging it into cold water, today's materials engineer adjusts the alloy's characteristics by rapid cooling. At cooling rates in excess of one million degrees per second it is possible to produce predictable microstructure in alloys. Such techniques are producing aluminium alloys with strength/weight characteristics better than titanium alloys. One of the rapid cooling techniques is to use high power lasers passed over a metal's surface. Using pre-alloyed powder, this laser-glazing process can construct complex shapes with great strength and temperature resistance.

While advanced metals are produced by adjusting alloy mixes and tailoring processing to obtain the required characteristics, composite materials are artificial constructions to produce materials with desired qualities. An early composite was fibreglass-reinforced plastic. This now familiar repair material for car bodywork uses the very high tensile strength of spun glass fibres reinforced in the matrix of the plastic bonding substance. The composite material has properties of strength and flexibility unknown in its components. Advanced composites take this process into new materials. The strength and stiffness of the composite is determined by the reinforcing material. Single fibres or whiskers of substances like glass, silicon carbide and aluminium oxide show greater strength than large pieces because, at the size of single crystals, they have fewer flaws. By bundling the fibres together, like bamboo canes, they add their strength together. If one breaks, the others take the load. The matrix material holds the bundles of fibres in the desired configuration. While fibreglass consisted of short fibres embedded in polyester, the advanced composites are arranged in a rigid polymer structure which gives much greater strength. Resins which can survive temperatures in excess of 300°C have now been developed. For higher temperatures, a metal matrix offers advantages. Arranging the fibres in the metal gives rise to considerable manufacturing difficulties but metal-matrix composites will undoubtedly have a role in medium to high temperature structures of the future. At the highest temperatures, ceramic matrix materials offer great promise. Borosilicate glass reinforced with silicon carbide fibres retains its strength at 1,000°C, with more exotic mixes operating up to 1,700°C.[3] Manufacture is difficult because the ceramic materials are themselves heat resistant. For even higher temperatures, the use of carbon-carbon composite material is possible. Here graphite crystals form the fibres, with amorphous carbon as the matrix. These advanced composites will allow considerable reduction in weights of aircraft structures. They offer better strength to weight, better stiffness, improved fatigue characteristics, greater fracture resistance and good thermal shock tolerance.

The new materials considered above have applications far wider than just aerospace, but the benefits in that field will drive research. New materials are not just offering replacements for old. In some areas new capabilities are offered by new materials. The transmission and processing of information has depended on electrical conductors in the past. The electrical conductivity of copper has made it a key commodity. New materials are changing this. In electrical conductivity, the possibilities of superconductors operating at near ambient temperatures promise enormous developments. The use of fibre optics to conduct information by photons instead of electrons also offers considerable military advantage.

Looking first at the new superconducting materials, it is now proving possible to produce ceramic materials which exhibit superconductivity at liquid nitrogen temperatures, and the prospect exists for such effects at even higher temperatures. In 1987, researchers at the

University of Houston developed a compound of yttrium, barium and copper oxide that superconducts at 90°C above absolute zero.[4] The loss of all electrical resistance at temperatures close to absolute zero has been known for the past two decades. High-power permanent electromagnets, new forms of computer memory, lossless power transmission and low level magnetic detection all become possible. While the energy costs of cooling conductors to these low temperatures have tended to outweigh the benefits in the past, we may now be moving into an era where superconducting ceramic materials affect a wide range of military activities. Superconducting computer components will offer increases in speed and power. Superconducting electric motors may at last replace the internal combustion engine. Sensors for magnetic anomalies and for electromagnetic radiation will be much more powerful. In this area the civil implications of mass-produced warm superconducting material will ensure that research continues.

In the processing of information, the use of photons has become possible through fibre optic systems. Lasers can produce small discrete pulses of light which are conducted in analagous ways to electrical signals. The very high frequencies associated with light make the information-carrying capacity orders of magnitude greater. Already the advantages of fibre optic communications from a security aspect are being utilized by the military. Jamming is much more difficult, information delivery rate is much higher and interception much harder. Photonic communications technology is advancing well but work is necessary to improve the laser sources used. More information could be carried if suitable emission and detection systems which used frequency-modulated light were developed. Current technology depends on straight pulsing. The detection electronics must also be able to cope with the very high switch rates of a photonic system, and further development work is necessary.[5]

In the field of electronics, materials technology also has much to offer. Semiconductors have led from transistors to integrated circuits of ever higher component density. Today, chips containing two million components are possible. Using silicon, the theoretical limit is about 100 million components per chip, and this density would appear achievable within the decade. To achieve faster processing it will be necessary to move to new materials, such as gallium arsenide, and new material structures of a three-dimensional arrangement. At this stage the work on photonic transmission and integrated circuits will begin to come together towards the photonic integrated circuit using photonic switches instead of transistor elements. Prototypes already exist. The increasing use of glass fibre communication systems will ensure that research in this field has a commercial incentive. It is likely that the development of photonic switches controlled by photonic signals will lead to the development of very high speed, high capacity information-processing systems.

Looking to the military implications of the many new areas for materials technology, it is clear that it is a crucial area. In the construction of weapon platforms, new materials will allow aircraft to fly faster, tanks to survive attacks better, ships to stay longer at sea and submarines to range further. Reduced size for performance will reduce detectability, and materials which absorb rather than reflect radars can be built in to the design. Jet engines which can operate at higher temperatures produce greater efficiency and thrust. Communications will be more assured, and information density greater. New computing power will become available for weapon guidance, control and information-processing. New sensors will make detection of the enemy much easier by day and by night.

At the same time these exotic materials are more difficult to manufacture, and require individual design for each component. This can make them very expensive to produce and to replace. In any new design it will be necessary to weigh the advantages against the cost. Battle damage repair is much easier to complete in traditional materials. Indeed new materials designed for the stresses of routine operating parameters may be weaker than normal metals in unpredictable combat conditions. The tale is still told of the corrosion proof fibreglass car which turns to powder on impact. The winning weapon must be robust as well as powerful.

In space, the new materials will assume yet greater importance. Indeed it has been the need to develop materials to cope with the heat of re-entry into the earth's atmosphere which has prompted much of the research. The reduction of weight, increase in strength and increase in engine performance will blur the distinction between air and space.

CHAPTER 11

Biotechnology

THE USE of organisms in warfare has a long, if inglorious, history. In 1346 the Mongols used plague corpses to infect the defenders in the seige of Caffa. The disease spread rapidly in the confined town, and the inhabitants were overcome. The British used smallpox patients' blankets as a gift to American Indians in 1763, and produced the desired effect of the spread of the disease among the tribes. The use of the anthrax organism was considered by the Allies in World War II. Tests were carried out in 1941 and 1942 on Gruinard Island off Scotland. The organism was so potent and hardy that it was only in 1988 that the island was declared safe for unprotected humans.[1]

Biological warfare (BW) has been waged with limited success on a few isolated occasions. While it potentially offers great killing power for small investment, the results have been unpredictable and unreliable. We are now moving into an age where developments in biotechnology offer the prospect of designing organisms for specific tasks, and this has significant military implications. An organism feeds on specific substances as nutrients, converts them to other substances, and multiplies under the right conditions. For thousands of years the ability of the yeast organism to feed on fruit sugar and convert it to ethanol has been used to the benefit of the winemaker—and wine drinker. Alcohol can also be used as a fuel, and yeast offers the prospect of strategic independence from oil suppliers. In World War I, starch was fermented with a bacterium to produce acetone and butanol which were needed for the munitions industry. Organisms can help nations at war both as offensive weapons and also as new sources of supply of strategic materials.

To see why biological warfare is becoming a more threatening possibility, it is first necessary to look at the current state of biotechnology, and then at the future possibilities. Mankind had used genetic engineering of a sort for thousands of years in producing crops of a singular strain, and selectively breeding animals for particular qualities. It was not until 1953 that the method by which such genetic qualities are passed on to successive generations was discovered. Francis Crick and James Watson explained how genetic information was stored and replicated through the double helix structure of the Deoxyribonucleic Acid (DNA) molecule. Nucleic acids, of which DNA is one, are found in all living organisms, and play the key role in the transmission of hereditary characteristics. It took another two decades for this research to develop into successful genetic engineering: manipulating genetic codes to provide specialized organisms. The process involves the insertion of genetic information into an organism, which is usually a bacterium, to give it new capabilities. Subsequent research has developed methods for designing and arranging the building blocks of DNA into a required structure. Whereas the early synthesis of human insulin required genetic material from human cells, it can now be entirely artificially constructed.[2]

Biotechnology is a young science but already the potential is vast. On first consideration it might appear that, for the military, the biological warfare possibilities are the most serious aspects to examine. If the scientist can design the organism to have specified characteristics, surely this offers an efficient method of killing the enemy? Before accepting this hypothesis, it is worth considering why biological warfare has been so limited in the past, and what new qualities agents would need to make it more successful in the future. An unclassified US military manual,[3] although over thirty years old, gives an excellent insight into the requirements of BW agents. BW differs from other combat methods by being entirely anti-personnel. Indeed it sets out to achieve what the popular Press claimed for the neutron bomb: killing people not property. That killing can be achieved by disease, through micro-organisms directly or indirectly from vectors such as insects, by toxins produced by organisms, or by the yet more indirect method of killing livestock or crops.

The essential requirements of BW agents are: consistency in effect; ease of production; stability in store; ease of dissemination; and stability after dissemination. Depending on its particular role, a BW agent will need a number of other qualities: short incubation period; appropriate persistence; difficulty of detection; resistance to countermeasures with easy self-protection. Anthrax, as we have seen, has long persistence and stability, but this becomes a disadvantage to friendly troops if the area is dangerous for forty years. It has a relatively short incubation period (1–7 days) but this is a long time in any modern war. It would be unfortunate if a ceasefire were agreed after three days' fighting, and the next day one side began to have 25 per cent deaths from anthrax. Indeed the question of the period from delivery to the onset of incapacity is crucial. It is possible to imagine a BW agent which is slow to act but is also rapidly spread by cross-infection being used in an undeclared war. The problem would be that the forces delivering the weapon would in due course be at risk from it.

The annual spread of influenza around the world is an example of how all mankind is vulnerable to highly infectious diseases. The state wishing to use such a weapon could take protective measures for its own population, but these would be difficult to hide, and could be taken as evidence of hostile action. Such a weapon is more likely to appeal to terrorist organizations. Looking to the future it is possible that viruses could be tailored to attack particular ethnic groups by using the differences in gene frequencies among the target population.[4] Also possible would be weapons which would attack the genetic material of the target rather than producing disease or poisoning by producing toxins. These genetic weapons would again have only long term effects, and therefore no place on the tactical battlefield.

Indeed given total freedom to design a battlefield bacteriological weapon, it is difficult to see what tactical advantages it offers over chemical weapons.[5] Incubation and incapacitating periods would be reduced to a minimum but are unlikely to reach the few seconds for CW agents or the near instantaneous effect of conventional weaponry. The spreading of disease can become a problem to friendly forces, and the long-term effects may be unpredictable. The protective measures taken against chemical weapons will also be effective against BW agents. The only significant advantage would be in the psychological effects. It might be that soldiers and civil populations under attack from disease would suffer greater stress than those vulnerable to more traditional killing systems. The international horror of biological warfare can also reduce the incentive to develop capabilities in this field. As there are few gains to be made from the use of such weapons in combat, military leaders should endorse moves towards arms control in this area.

If BW is of limited use, even with genetically engineered agents, can it be discounted? Unfortunately the strategic, covert, long-term use of micro-organisms is a real threat. If an agent can be tailored to kill a particular population group, undeclared war could be waged most effectively. The spread of the HTLV-III AIDS virus provides an example of how a long-term agent can spread exponentially. In the case of AIDS the discrimination is caused by methods of infection. The ethnic weapons suggest that targeting might be much more selective. Alternatively, economic war might be waged by targeting the main food crop of a particular nation with a particular virus. These possibilities offer particularly effective warfare for terrorist groups as well as unethical states.

The prospects are not entirely negative, however. As the technology to design destructive agents increases, so also does the ability to manufacture vaccines and other protective measures. The difficulty should not be underrated, and the case of AIDS again illustrates the time it

takes. Nevertheless, genetic engineering will provide protective vaccines and toxoids. It will provide protection in other ways as well. The
characteristic of an organism to feed on a given nutrient, and convert
it to another substance, can be used to make very sensitive and selective sensors. These biosensors will be engineered to act as rapid and
cheap chemical agent detectors. The protective measures against
chemical and biological agents are of no use unless they are deployed
in time. The biosensors will be able to detect such small concentrations
in such rapid time that effective protective measures can be taken.

It is conceivable that these micro-organism sensors could be developed to detect other militarily significant emissions. If we think of the
biosensor as feeding on a few specified molecules, and amplifying its
output through a cascade of suitable organisms, then it becomes an
extremely sensitive "nose". Could this sniffer detect gases from a submerged submarine, or smell out hidden troops, or tell a missile
whether it was about to strike a friendly or enemy aricraft? None of
this is any more unlikely than the ability of a dog to find drugs or
explosives on the basis of a few molecules of escaping vapour.

The developments in biotechnology will, for the most part, be
driven by the needs of the civilian sector. In the medical sphere this
will be in the prevention and cure of disease, and hence have a direct
benefit to the military requirement both for protection and for rapid
healing of casualties. In the industrial field, the early work on production of fuel from sugar by fermentation points to the prospect of
new fuel sources. Genetic engineering offers the prospect of designing a yeast that feeds on cellulose to produce alcohol. It would then
be able to make fuel directly from all plant material. This would make
a nation independent of oil supplies. When the military first started
worrying about the finite nature of oil, following the 1973 crisis,
schemes for using hydrogen instead of oil abounded. The difficulty
was the high energy requirements to extract hydrogen by electrolysis
from water. It may prove to be possible to extract hydrogen molecules
from water by growing a genetically engineered algae or bacteria.

Microbes are already being used in industrial processes to concentrate minerals, clean up pollutants and synthesize plastics. The techniques for extraction of metals from low grade ores using microbes
may offer cheap methods for obtaining weapon grade uranium. The
Stanrock Uranium Mine in Canada uses bacteria to leach uranium
oxide from rock without mining the ore. The required mineral
accumulates in pools where it can be readily collected.[6] It is possible
to conceive of the military use of a microbe which would be designed
to eat strategic material. If rapidly-breeding bacteria which decom-
posed stainless steel or plastic or protective clothing were used on an
enemy and its equipment the results could be catastrophic. However,

if the organism were long-lived and rapid breeding, it would soon become a threat to both sides in a conflict. If it were not it is likely that conventional forms of attack would be more effective. It seems that whenever biological offensive methods are considered, the same problems in usage arise.

Biotechnology is also moving towards electronics and photonics in the realm of computing. The limit on component density in conventional silicon chip-type technology is within sight, as we explore in the next Chapter. Photonics offer one method of increasing chip density and computing speeds and power. The brain shows that organisms can achieve very much higher packing densities. While the possibility of producing artificial brains is beyond the timescale considered here, biochips are possible in the relatively near term.

The ability to design protein molecules which are organized in pre-determined three dimensional structures gives the prospect of growing circuits. Semiconductor molecules would be included in the protein framework. The biochip could then be self-reproducing, regenerative and of high capacity. Militarily, the added advantage could be resistance to electromagnetic pulse effects, as well as very compact size for given capacity.

It is clear from the wide range of possible developments in biotechnology that it is an area of research which merits considerable effort. Many of the developments will be achieved by commercial pressures. However, while civil techniques will be usable by the military, there will be a need for considerable defence investment. In particular, the use of biosensors is likely to be of greatly increased importance. In the longer term the biochip may be an important advance in computer technology. As to biological offensive warfare, there is little to suggest that genetic engineering offers a war-winning weapon. The threat of covert use of biological agents must be countered. This will be partly a question of intelligence and partly defensive measure research: a field for civil and military co-operation.

CHAPTER 12

Electronics

THE IMPORTANCE of electronics in defence is recognized by the now commonplace term Electronic Warfare (EW). However EW is only one area where developments in electronics are significant. In Chapter 6 the importance of new electronic solid state devices to computing was explored. In the home today, electronic devices bring entertainment, cook the food, wash the clothes, answer the phone and add up the bills. At the office, decisions are made on the basis of electronic analysis. The written word from memo to book is electronically composed, edited, copied and published. Communications are virtually instantaneous and worldwide.

Electronics is the applied science which deals with the control of electrons. The early use of electromagnetic wave propagation, with tuned spark oscillators and germanium diode (cat's whisker) detectors, led to the development of modern radio communications. The solid state diode gave way to the thermionic valve as an amplifying device. In turn, the valve has given way to the transistor and its development into integrated circuits. The requirements of electronic circuits to control electron flow have remained, and have been tackled in different ways. Ever weaker signals can be detected: more powerful signals can be transmitted over a greater and greater range of frequencies; control becomes faster, uses less power and is more reliable. In this Chapter we consider the developments in the civil and military field which will affect the use of the electromagnetic spectrum in the future.

At the lowest end of the frequency spectrum are the radio frequencies. Since the invention of the triode valve at the start of the twentieth century, the range of radio frequencies and amount of information that can be carried has expanded significantly. The characteristics of these frequencies have been exploited for military purposes. Low frequencies can carry little information, but can travel great distances and penetrate solid material. Extra Low Frequency (ELF) communications have little to offer the civilian market but are of great importance for long-range strategic communications—particularly to submarines.[1] For this reason research into improving rate of information transfer, robustnessness of the vast aerial arrays necessary and reception systems will be crucially important.

Moving into the more familiar regions of the very low frequency to ultra-high frequency (UHF) radio spectrum (10 kc/s to 1,000 Mc/s) the air waves are crammed with many users. At the low end of the range, domestic radio competes with navigational systems. The use of worldwide navigation systems based on radio waves is of considerable importance to military operations. While internal navigational sys- tems based on inertial platforms can be remarkably accurate, they will not provide the required precision for long-distance weapon delivery. Radio navigation systems provide external reference but have disad- vantages from their vulnerability to enemy attack or electronic inter- ference. They also offer the enemy navigational benefits. Alternative avenues of approach to the navigational problem include computer matching of terrain characteristics. Typically, a radar picture will be matched to stored information to provide a navigational update. This requires the aircraft or missile to emit a radar signal which may in itself be vulnerable to countermeasures. Research into encoded reliable external navigational aids has therefore some potential, and is explored later in this Chapter.

Moving up the spectum to the High Frequency (HF)—or short wave—region we are at the busiest, currently most useful and least reliable, long-range radio communication bands. The curious phenomenon that electromagnetic radiation of particular frequencies is reflected back to earth by ionised layers in the upper atmosphere led to worldwide communications. HF can achieve reasonably high rates of information transfer over vast distances. It is, however, not totally predictable, can be easily intercepted and is prone to counter- measures. Modern technology offers the ability to select optimum frequencies, switch between them rapidly for security, encode the information and compress transmissions to minimize detection time.[2] The miniaturizing of electronic components is important in making such communication equipment useful on the battlefield. Research is still needed to produce a reliable battlefield communi- cation system which will allow interchange of both data and com- mands between all elements of forces in the air and on the ground. The propagation characteristics of HF have also led to the develop- ment of Over The Horizon (OTH) radar. With vast aerial arrays under the right conditions, low level targets can be detected some 1,800 miles away.[3]

For every use of the electromagnetic spectrum, there is always the possibility of a countermeasure. EW includes the interception of sig- nals to provide intelligence. The nature of the signal (frequency, power, source, data type polarization, duration) in itself provides intelligence. If the data carried can also be understood then yet more intelligence flows. For tactical battlefield communications, locating a major radio source may identify the location of headquarters, which can then be targeted. A command network can be jammed to cause confusion, or can be deceived by spoof transmissions. In turn the active EW enemy can have his jamming systems used as sources for information. The EW battle is a complex one of measure, counter-measure and counter-countermeasure.

The VHF and UHF bands have the advantages of offering reliable communication with high data density, but can only do this over line of sight orders of range. For communications within battle formations or from aircraft this is useful, but it makes the wider command and control more difficult. The use of land-based relay stations, while effective, is costly in manpower and makes any network vulnerable. The use of airborne relay systems extends range, but requires constant patrol of relay aircraft. Space-based satellite relay is the obvious choice for providing long-range reliable communications, and their use was discussed in Chapter 8. However the vulnerability of satellites in the future suggests that it would be unwise to rely exclusively on such systems. A number of choices suggest themselves when looking for invulnerable high altitude reflectors that are sufficiently robust to enemy action. The moon is a large reflector available to a wide area of the earth at any given time. The use of rebroadcast systems could be effective, but they could also be destroyed by radiation-homing weapon systems of the future. More reliable would be the development of suitable signal-processing systems that could use the very weak reflected signals 'bounced' off the surface of the moon. Another possibility might be the development of localized atmospheric layers with the required reflection characteristics. These might be initiated by rockets launched to the required height dispersing a form of chaff or a suitable chemical seed to induce the required ionisation layer. Reflecting balloons, or rebroadcasting balloons, might be another productive area.

As the frequency of the electromagnetic waves increases, it can carry more information, but can be obstructed more easily. The development of radar was explored in the first part of this book. It is vital to every area of warfare today. To detect enemy aircraft, missiles, ships, tanks, guns; to identify friendly forces; to identify targets or compute position and altitude. The enormous range of radar-associated military tasks makes it a prime area for research into countermeasures. Radar has been improved by narrower beam width and higher frequency for greater discrimination. The reflected signal can also be analysed for any Doppler shift in frequency caused by relative movement. The advent of moving target discrimination has made aircraft radars much more effective in the look-down mode. By isolating the moving target returns, the background clutter from reflected signals from the ground is eliminated. Signal-processing techniques allow detailed pictures to be built up of objects reflecting radar illumination. Identification is a key concern for military radar systems. The use of the radar signal to trigger a coded radar response (as in Identification Friend or Foe, IFF) is widely used for both commercial and military aircraft. It has many weaknesses and would not be of much use in the electronic warfare environment of the future. It may be possible for the radar system to be much more discriminate, or to be coupled to sensors of other frequencies, and to compare returns with appropriate identification algorithms. These could lead to an intelligent radar able to give much higher assurance of correct identification.

The mechanics of radar are also undergoing a transformation. The use of steerable dishes to direct the beam is giving way to much more rapidly responding phased array radars.[4] In these, a flat regular array of radiating elements are fed with radar signals which produce interference patterns as the waves reinforce or cancel each other. By controlling the time at which an element sends its signal, the relative phases change and the effective direction of reinforced signals is altered. The narrow beam can be steered in this way and achieve very rapid switching rates. This allows it to cover a wide area and a large number of targets. The lack of moving mechanical parts makes the system lighter and more reliable for a given performance. New developments should lead to the production of integrated circuits which would provide the phase shifters, switchers and amplifiers for each radiating element on a single chip with the necessary microprocessor control. With that order of miniaturization, radar performance for all weapon systems will be much enhanced.

The counters to developments in radar are also of interest to the researcher. Signals can be obscured by jamming or by decoy returns such as chaff. The computational power being developed allows the illuminating radar signal to be detected and processed to feed back false information. For example it could be frequency-shifted to indicate false velocity vectors, or phase-shifted to give incorrect or ambiguous range data; or simply overloaded. Much development work is also going into reducing the radar signature of potential targets. This can be done by using radar-absorbent materials, shaping the structure appropriately, and reducing surface area. This stealth technology can reduce radar cross-sections but will not make targets invisible to radar. For the future, greater use of decoys may be necessary. Current generation decoys are expendable and relatively short-lived. It may be that aircraft will fly in formation with electronic drones, tanks will be hidden among small motorized electronic radar stand-ins, and ships will sail with a flotilla of electronic surrogates.

As the frequency increases yet further, the millimetric radar region, with its yet greater target discrimination, gives way to infra-red radiation. Infra-red (IR) has been used in the past for terminal guidance for missiles, viewing targets at night, reconnaissance, and intelligence from heat distribution patterns. So far the difficulty with infra-red detectors has been their requirement for low temperature cooling and their extreme fragility. Just as the phased-array radar is transforming the cumbersome radar tracker, so solid state sensors which can be scanned are transforming infra-red sensors. The improvement in sensitivity and robustness makes for much more effective missile guidance systems. The IR missile can either home on to a hot spot on the target, such as the jet efflux, or can home on to a suitable target designator illumination, such as a laser-illuminated spot. Each system spawns its countermeasure with such devices as IR jammers. However, coupling high resolution with computer-matching of target images will make the well-aimed IR missile difficult to fool in days to come. Using infra-red radiation as an extension of visible light will also be improved by increasing development of sensor technology. Already Forward-Looking Infra-Red (FLIR) gives a good night low-level capability to high-speed military aircraft. As the speed of processing of information is increased and the sensors become more sensitive, aircraft will be able to fly yet lower and faster. If the picture is also compared to terrain data held in computer memory, it should be possible to use it for navigation and target acquisition. The passive nature of infra-red sensors makes them less vulnerable to enemy detection.

As the infra-red gives way to the visible light spectrum, technology has already improved the soldier's eyes immeasurably. The telescope and binoculars were rapidly adopted to make the enemy more easily visible, and smoke and camouflage followed as countermeasures. Visible light remains a key area of the electromagnetic spectrum for exploitation. Surveillance in the past depended on photographic recording. This is still available, particularly from satellite strategic reconnaissance systems but, for tactical information, infra-red and radar systems have taken over. Electronic enhancement through low light television and night vision devices have made operations in the dark possible. The laser operating in the visible and near visible region has allowed target illumination. The laser also offers the possibility of high-density data transmission. The use of fibre optics to carry the laser signal reduces attenuation and can give high security from interference and interception. Developments involving the alignment of two conventional semiconductor lasers have produced beams of almost perfect purity. These cleaved-coupled-cavity lasers can carry data at rates of one thousand million bits per second. This equates to transmitting the entire text of the *Encyclopaedia Britannica* in less than half a second, with an error of no more than one letter.[5] The use of light for communication will undoubtedly increase as the need for data transfer increases and concerns about countermeasures mount. Lasers may also have a role in overhead reconnaissance from aircraft or satellites. Successful experiments in detection of submarines through laser waveform interference[6] point the way ahead.

Solid state technology can provide night vision goggles which make it safe to fly visually in very poor ambient light levels at low level. As the power of these devices is developed further, and mass production becomes feasible, it is conceivable that every soldier could operate equally well by day as by night. This would have significant implications for the battlefield, which is already well on the way to being a continuous 24-hour a day operation.

Beyond the visible region of the spectrum lie the ultraviolet, X-rays, gamma rays and cosmic rays. The uses of these regions are as yet relatively unexplored. In Chapter 5 some of the possibilities of the high energy particles at these frequencies were touched upon, and in Chapter 7 the selective radiations from third-generation nuclear weapons were discussed. It may be that pure research in these regions will suggest ways in which such radiation may be applied in communication or surveillance. For instance, neutrinos have the ability to pass through the earth with only slight attenuation. This suggests that if a suitable detector were available, it would be possible to 'X-ray' the earth and its oceans from space. It is difficult to see how such a detector might be constructed but neutrino detection research is carried out by astronomers now.

This Chapter has concentrated on the exploitation of the electromagnetic spectrum for military use. Major advances will come from the application of the new computing capabilities to the processing of the electronic data.[7] By combining information from different parts of the spectrum, processing it to enhance the image and comparing to stored known characteristics, high quality resolution will be possible. The soldier in the trench with a handheld air-to-air missile needs an interlock to prevent him firing at friendly targets. The aircraft with the beyond-visual range missile needs positive identification of his target. The detection of enemy communications needs instant analysis to provide appropriate reaction. The communication network needs to be able to analyse countermeasures and automatically adjust itself to restore data exchange. The high-level commander needs to have the information from all the different sensor sources analysed and presented in an understandable form.[8]

The developments on so many fronts in electronics might make it possible to thin the fog of war a little. The pilot on his way to the target, at low level in the dark, would see the terrain as clearly as in daylight. Superimposed on it would be threat-information derived from space, air and ground sensors. He would have his own forces clearly distinguished from the enemy. The targets would be highlighted in order of importance. At the same time his sensors would feed back into the information network. Countermeasures to all this would also be a ripe area for research.

Research must also look at exploiting other ways of carrying out the tasks now done by traditional electromagnetic radiation methods. Sonar has long given an equivalent to radar under the sea. The new developments in signal-processing will improve its capability. The low end of the radio frequency can penetrate the sea for communication; can it offer any detection possibilities despite the very long wavelengths? Already, over the horizon, radar techniques are becoming practical.

In the field of electronics, military technology will remain specialized, but will gain its major advances from both pure research and from commercial imperatives in the electronics industry.

This review of the implications of electronics research for future military capabilities concludes the second part of the book. Having looked at lessons from the past, examined the possibilities of today, we examine the possible battles of the future in the concluding section.

Part Three – War in the Future

CHAPTER 13

The Sea–Air Battle

WHAT IS the sea–air battle of the future to be like? We saw in the first part of the book how certain technological advances, such as torpedoes, submarines and radar transformed the nature of maritime warfare. Today, we can watch the oceans from space, we can send guided missiles over thousands of miles with pinpoint accuracy, and the seas have lost the exclusive role they had as international lines of communication. On the other hand, the oceans are now far more important in the economic resource area, with ever greater development of underwater oil fields and the promise of mineral exploitation from the deep sea bed. While air transport has blossomed over the past thirty years, sea cargo is still the major contributor to long-distance haulage. In this Chapter we shall try to extrapolate the trends in maritime operations (below, on and above the sea), and in the light of the possible technological advances already examined, propose possible schemes for effective development.

Considering first future strategic nuclear systems, the continuing viability of the submarine-based ballistic missile is of prime importance. The missile itself will need to be developed as necessary to counter any developing strategic defensive systems. This is unlikely to be an insurmountable problem, given the technological problems in developing totally reliable ballistic missile defences. The developments required for the missile are likely to be navigation systems, which are independent of external systems, as satellites become more vulnerable to attack; defences; and short flight times to reduce exposure time to defensive weapons. It is unlikely that cruise missile systems will become more attractive than ballistic missiles for strategic deterrence. Their slow speeds will make countermeasures easier to develop and, when used against strategic forces, they allow too much time for enemy systems to be reloaded or moved.

The major uncertainty over the strategic nuclear submarine of the future is how well hidden it can remain. Large as the oceans are, they represent a finite volume for detection. The detection methods available include satellite and aircraft reconnaissance through the increasing range of sensors which are being developed, surface ship-controlled sensor systems, hunter submarines and remote underwater sensors. All these systems are likely to be needed in the future and the sensitivity of sensor systems will be improved markedly. Possible research areas which may bear fruit will include the use of high energy lasers as a form of underwater radar, computer developments to improve the picture that can be built up from sonar and other sensors, the use of new types of sensing for gases emitted, disturbances in the water temperature or pressures and, speculatively, the detection of high energy particle scatter through the earth. It seems, however, that rendering the sea transparent at all times is a formidable problem. As sensors improve, so the ability to conceal the submarine will also improve. For the foreseeable future it is likely that submarines will offer the best base for strategic retaliatory forces to remain secure.

One outstanding difficulty with strategic submarine forces is the requirement for reliable and effective command and control arrangements. In the area of communications there remains considerable scope for progress. It may be that lasers will offer some scope for deep water communications from satellite stations. Another vulnerability of the submarine which tries to remain hidden is its need to return to port at the end of each patrol. It is when entering and departing from the home base that it is at greatest risk and the opportunity to trail it arises. As trailing techniques improve this may become a limitation.

Despite these concerns for the future, the submarine will remain a key feature of any war at sea in the future. The historical evidence of its importance in conflicts is valid for the future. The attack submarine will be a growing part of nations' forces. The advantages of nuclear power in ability to remain submerged are great, but the cost will also remain very high. It may be that developments in fuel technology will make the non-nuclear submarine a better buy, if it can achieve the necessary range without having to surface.

If the submarine is going to be an increasingly widespread threat, then the importance of anti-submarine warfare will be undiminished in the future. Forces today devote considerable resources to this area of warfare. The enemy submarine must be detected, and this may be done by another submarine, by surface ships or from the air. The problem is so great that it will normally require elements of many different systems, as will the destruction of the submarine. In the future, detection will remain the key to successful anti-submarine warfare operations. A combination of sensors from satellites to sonar will still be required. Increases in computing power will give greater discrimination to long-distance sonar systems, and provide effective noise filters. In the battle against the submarine, the possibility of novel weapon systems is real. The drone has become an interesting development in air warfare. It has parallel possibilities in naval oper-

ations. An intelligent drone might patrol the important sea lanes, with
the possibility of relaying information or even launching attacks on
hostile submarines. Removing the man from the attack submarine
would allow it to be much smaller and cheaper.

The protection offered by the sea could also be exploited in the
development of new roles for submarines. The use of small submarines for behind-the-lines reconnaissance has a stirring history, and
future midget submarines might be allocated target designation and
infiltration roles. In weapon systems, the growing intelligence of torpedoes will allow longer ranges for fire-and-forget systems. Mines
should invariably be controllable externally, so that minefields can be
neutralized for friendly operations, and selectively fused for offensive
and defensive operations. These mines could be given some freedom
of movement both in depth and position, as a counter to mine-sweep-
ing systems.

If technology will be important to the war beneath the waves, what
of the future for surface ships in conflict? In Chapter 2 we examined
the historical developments of maritime warfare, and the increasing
vulnerability of surface fleets to technological improvements. The
ship is a relatively large, slow-moving, valuable target. The ethos of
navies derives from the 'all of one company' environment: when a
ship sinks, the Captain is as vulnerable as the most junior rating.
There is no natural cover or refuge, although in the past the very
vastness of the oceans has hidden fleets—for a time at least.

It would seem entirely possible that a space-based radar reconnaissance system, coupled to large computer information-processing systems, would allow nations to maintain an up-to-date picture of the
locations and movements of all the surface shipping in the world. If
such a system were tied into an appropriate anti-ship long-range missile system, the near simultaneous elimination of an enemy fleet might
become feasible. Such a comprehensive anti-ship weapon system
would not be cheap but could more readily be achieved than a perfect
ballistic missile defence. In any such development, countermeasures
would be sought: radar decoys, anti-satellite weapons, jamming, and
passive and active defences against the incoming missiles. Covering
the surface of the earth would require the use of ballistic missiles of
strategic capability. The launch of a large number of these weapons
simultaneously against an enemy navy could, and probably would, be
taken as an attempt at a pre-emptive nuclear strike. It is possible,
therefore, to envisage a vastly expensive counter-ship worldwide missile system which could never be used for fear of starting a nuclear
war.

The more realistic future development would be the deployment
of a space-based ocean surveillance system, with a high degree of

redundancy, which can keep track of surface shipping, and relay the information by data link directly to local forces, in the air or the sea or on land. The sensors can be derived from a number of the new technologies considered. For surface ships, radar with signal-processing will continue to be the primary system. Countermeasures for the ship will include the reduction in radar signature through shape design and materials which absorb rather than reflect the radar signals. The size and complexity of naval surface ships is unlikely to make these techniques sufficient on their own. However, if the radar signature can be reduced at the same time as more active deceptive measures are taken, the reconnaissance problem is made much more difficult. Jamming, by saturation of the radar frequencies in use, can backfire if the attacker has a 'home-on-jam' (using the jamming signal itself to identify the target) facility. More fruitful may be the refinement of deceptive electronic warfare techniques. The processing and retransmission of the radar signal to build up a false picture of the target is increasingly made possible through high speed computing. The processing time must be short, with radar signals travelling at the speed of light. It is possible to imagine the very high-speed computer—possibly through photonic, superconducting or biotechnology—being able to follow frequency-agile radars at sufficient speed to analyse and reconstruct the signal, and transmit it back sufficiently rapidly to fool the detection-processing system. A battle of computing power would then be waged, as the radar-operating system attempted to extract more and more data in the ever shorter time available before the target captured and modified the return signal.

Radar is not the only means of detection of surface ships. While it will provide the best system, the rest of the electromagnetic spectrum is available where it can penetrate the atmosphere. In particular, a combination of highly sensitive and discriminating infra-red detection with radar would make a powerful combination. When conditions permitted, these sources would be supplemented by visible light detection. Indeed the passive sensors could be used whenever possible, with the advantage that they are less likely to trigger defensive countermeasures. Radar would then be available as a supplementary identifier. If countermeasures make its information ambiguous, a laser system using technologies for long-range laser propagation in the atmosphere, developed in strategic defence research, could be used for confirmation. On balance, the new technologies are moving towards making it more and more difficult to hide the surface fleet.

Given this picture of increasing vulnerability, there are a number of avenues which may merit investigation. The first is to accept a reducing role for surface ships in any future conflict. Other ways of carrying out their tasks should be found. A primary role is the transport of large quantities of men and supplies. In theory, these could either go above or below the oceans. In practice, the quantities of loads make air transport impossible for all but a fraction. We explore future air transport options in Chapter 15, but it suffices to say that technology as yet offers no prospect of replacing sea cargo by air cargo. This presupposes that gravity remains a one-way force. Cargo haulage under the sea might be worth greater effort. Technology already allows submarines of very large displacements: the Soviet *Typhoon* class is of the order of 25,000 metric tons. The danger during loading and unloading would have to be considered. Underwater ports, mobile docks and submarine tenders would help to reduce the risks during these critical times.

Whether such an unusual approach to the problem would be a sensible investment would depend on the type of conflict expected. Currently, NATO depends heavily on reinforcement of Europe across the Atlantic. While the most important forces would move by air, a major part depends on sea transport. The effectiveness of such a reinforcement plan depends on the availability of sea transport, the time when the reinforcements are required, and when hostilities begin. If the assumption is made that reinforcement takes place in time of crisis, but before war breaks out, then surface merchant and naval shipping is an entirely sensible way to carry out the reinforcement task. Indeed, the highly visible form of transport has added deterrence advantages as a means of showing political resolve. If war has broken out, keeping the sea lines of communication open for such shipping becomes a vital and difficult task. It is by no means obvious which would be the most expensive way forward: adequate surface shipping and the necessary defensive measures, adequate air transport and the necessary defensive measures, or the development of a new submarine-transport capability and the required defended docking facilities. What would certainly be cheaper—and more effective—would be the pre-positioning of as much of the equipment as possible in the forward area, and the setting up of the necessary logistic support organization in the forward area. Air reinforcement would be available to bring the manpower forward when necessary, and would act as the political signal in crisis management. The defence of the Falkland Islands is organized on this basis now. Although technology appears to offer a partial solution, it would be at high cost; a lower cost solution with no technical risk already exists. This does solve the problem of equipment being in the wrong place, or having to be duplicated against a number of different scenarios. Nevertheless, it is often possible to pool equipment in continental storage areas where no subsequent cross-water deployment is necessary.

Even if such foresight allowed nations to fight without needing to defend the sea lines of communication, this would not mean that the oceans could be abandoned to the enemy. No amount of stockpiling of either war supplies or strategic materials can make a nation independent of sea transport. As we saw earlier, new materials and biotechnology may reduce this dependence but nations are growing more rather than less interdependent economically. The submarine threat will have to be countered and this will remain the priority for military technology.

It is, of course, possible that technology will change the nature of surface ships. Great excitement was generated by the development of the hovercraft, and some believed that it would have an increasing role to play in maritime warfare. Hovercraft are faster and more manoeuvrable than conventional ships, and have the major advantage that they can operate on both land and sea. This makes them well suited to amphibious operations. The Soviet Union has developed an air cushion vehicle with 350tons displacement for such operations. However, what seemed a significant advance has become an interesting specialist vehicle. The limitations of sea state, the vulnerability to system failure and the size limitations have offset the advantages of speed and sea/land capability in the minds of many. It may be that slow technical evolution in reliability and operating capability will tilt the balance of advantage towards air cushion vehicles in time.

Speed is an important characteristic in surface ships. Commercial pressures in competitive transport fields have led to the development of alternative faster systems of water transport. Systems generating lift in the water to reduce the drag of the hull have abounded, and hydrofoils are commonplace in the ports of the world. For rapid reaction to sea threats, they offer a useful capability, and could be armed with missile systems against sea and air targets. They are unlikely to be practical in sizes which would allow them to become the most significant vessels. Extrapolating the trend which led from sail, to steam, to aircraft carrier, to submarine as the power in the oceans, there seems no prospect of technical development which can place a form of surface ship as the next stage. The need is for smaller, faster, more potent and less vulnerable surface vessels.

At the same time there are pressures on navies to move towards reductions in manpower. The life of the sailor has always had disadvantages, and as the press gang has been replaced by the lure of high pay, the cost of manpower has been an increasing factor in overall costs. The unmanned intelligent naval drone may offer many attractions. In the early stages of development a manned mother ship, in safe waters, could launch and control such offensive and defensive long-range systems. When the enhancements in computing capability allow, such systems could become semi-autonomous. They would be given patrol areas, be able to detect potential targets, analyse and compare their characteristics, identify them as friendly or hostile, and take appropriate offensive or defensive action. The automated battlefield is often quoted as the way ahead for land/air warfare, and we discuss it in the next Chapter; but in many ways the oceans offer a more productive area for such developments. The delineation between the mine, the torpedo, the ship and the submarine will gradually disappear. Such systems do not, of course, solve the problems of naval warfare. The technology necessary to deceive them with countermeasures and the offensive warfare to destroy them will also develop in parallel.

Looking next at the air aspects of future maritime warfare, we must consider the missions that will be required, the vehicles that will be necessary and the way that technology will provide them. Aircraft are used for reconnaissance, offensive operations and defence of friendly maritime forces. These tasks will remain: however the balance between surface and subsurface operations may change. In the reconnaissance role, satellites have an increasingly important part to play, as already discussed. They will also become more vulnerable, and they lack the immediate follow-up offensive capability when a target is identified. Maritime patrol aircraft can examine smaller areas in considerable detail. As the technology improves the ability of sensors, and computing power improves analysis, the aircraft will remain an important element in clearing a particular sea area. It will itself be increasingly vulnerable to air defence systems. This suggests that reconnaissance drones may be important. However, the ability of aircraft to deploy rapidly to the tactical area will still be needed, and air-launched drones, with the main information-processing systems in the mother aircraft, may be the best balance of risk. Such systems will not be cheap, and the overall balance of investment between air reconnaissance sensors, satellite systems and land-based long-range detection will have to be considered closely. The satellite systems will have many applications in surveillance, and are likely to be important in peace, crisis management and transition to war, as well as in war itself. For those reasons, the level of maritime air reconnaissance effort may decline as the satellite systems improve. Much will depend on the technological development of long-range submarine detection. If laser interference methods from low-earth orbit—or other more exotic space-based methods—prove productive, the need for maritime reconnaissance aircraft will decrease. There is little prospect of that at present.

For offensive operations, the maritime attack aircraft will continue to be an important means of bringing firepower to bear quickly. The battle between defence and offence technologies will continue. At sea the variables are more easily quantified than in the land battle. Against an enemy surface fleet, the target is well defined and, if distant from land-based air defence, will have to depend on its own organic air defence. On the other hand, it is possible to concentrate air defence systems on the single task of protecting the fleet. The use of air-launched stand-off missiles to attack ships is already with us, as the use of the Exocet in the Falklands conflict made clear. Fast-reacting missile or gun-based defences are also well developed. Technology will therefore be working towards attack missiles which are more difficult to defeat. This can be through greater speed, stealth, electronic warfare or saturation of defences. The last might be achieved by the use of many smaller warheads with vulnerable point-seeking capability provided by greater intelligence. While in many cases surface-to-surface missiles, either launched from land bases or other ships or submarines, will provide a good capability against ships, and the submarine-launched torpedo will remain a potent weapon, aircraft systems will continue to have an important part to play. They combine quick response with extended range, and can give greater opportunity for target identification and discrimination.

In the anti-submarine war, it is entirely sensible to combine the offensive capability with the reconnaissance system. Once found by the aircraft sensors, the submarine can be attacked by air-launched torpedo systems. An agile aircraft will not be needed until the submarine has its own air defence capability. It is possible that providing such a capability could be a profitable field for development. Unfortunately, launch of an air defence missile by a submarine would give its location away. However, it could be used once the submarine had been located by the reconnaissance aircraft, or if the aircraft were operating independently as is likely to be the case. Certainly a submarine able to defend itself from the air threat would make the search task more difficult. The technical problems are great. The submarine has to be able to acquire and track the target aircraft while submerged, and without giving away its location. It might be that some form of sound detection system would offer the best avenue for research.

The air defence of the surface fleet is more easily provided. As discussed above, the relatively small target area makes point defence feasible through weapon systems designed to destroy incoming missiles. Electronic warfare advances will make the attacker's and defender's tasks more difficult. The use of sea-based air defence from aircraft carriers or VTOL aircraft from suitable ships is one element, although an increasingly expensive form. Land-based air defence requires considerable air-to-air refuelling support and is costly in aircraft numbers. However, these longer ranged aircraft offer more flexibility in employment, and can be used where the threat is greatest.

It may be that as the number of systems which can attack surface ships increase in quantity and quality, the traditional aim of a favourable air situation at sea will become unattainable. In these circumstances, those surface ships which must continue to operate will rely on terminal defence measures. These will be an enveloping protective screen to detect and destroy incoming warheads below the sea, in the water and through the air.

The detection screen will be provided on the ship, and on its escorts, but will have to extend further and further forward, as weapons are launched from greater ranges and at higher speeds, in turn decreasing response time. Already helicopters provide an extended detection system against the submarine threat. Airborne early-warning systems can detect enemy aircraft and must improve their capability to plot incoming missiles. The air, sea and sub-sea threat picture is built up from these many sources and, as the computing capability of the individual sensors and the central controlling system improve, such defensive systems may offer a reasonable level of protection.

It will be a difficult decision for governments. The cost of providing survivable surface shipping capability is already increasing to an extent that fleet numbers are declining. If the price of survival is an inability to continue to keep the sea lanes open, then the price may be too high. Technology does offer some prospects for reducing the operating costs of navies. Certainly new ships need to be more automated and less manpower-intensive. Also, the use of simulation could reduce dramatically the time needed at sea, and could improve the combat experience of crews. The experience of aircraft simulators has been extremely good, and the whole aircraft mission simulator, involving a complete crew, is now well established. The use of command simulators for naval warfare is also prevalent, and could be compared to the pilot's cockpit part of an aircraft simulator. What advanced computing could provide is a whole ship simulator. To be worthwhile, the operating navy would have to standardize on a number of the type of ship being simulated. The build costs would be high, but the advantages in both expertise and finance could be considerable. The prolonged sailing times in transit to exercise areas would be unnecessary, and a greater proportion of time would be spent on operational training. Combat training would be more realistic, and combat analysis more effective. The use of whole ship simulation has much to offer maritime powers in the future. To be effective, the simulator must be introduced at an early stage of the procurement process, and must be updated with the ship. This is expensive, and does not provide extra weaponry. Nevertheless the savings in training costs, coupled with the improvement in effectiveness, make it a worthwhile investment as computing technology allows a realistic simulation to be achieved for such a complex activity.

This review of the future direction of sea/air warfare has tended to suggest that changes will be of an incremental nature. The prophet always treads a difficult path between being over-cautious—depending on the lessons of yesterday—and being unrealistic by expecting too much of tomorrow. The realities of economic pressures favour an incremental approach to changes in the balance of maritime warfare. Nevertheless, it is important to consider what technological advances could change the nature of maritime warfare in a revolutionary way, and what steps should be taken now to minimize the risk.

If submarines could be detected, identified and destroyed with reasonable certainty, the balance of maritime power would change significantly. This is the key area for technological investment. We have seen some of the possible avenues for appropriate sensor systems and offensive weapons. If the technological breakthrough comes to make the oceans transparent, it is likely that the sensor system will need to be space-based to cover a sufficiently wide area. The best insurance, therefore, against such a breakthrough would be the development of anti-satellite weapons. The nature of these weapons is considered in Chapter 15. Even if the detection breakthrough were other than by overhead surveillance (perhaps a form of long-range underwater acoustic analysis), the communication and control is likely to depend on satellite systems and the same argument holds good. Against surface ships, it is likely to be a question of increasing vulnerability, as radar ranges extend. The production of large quantities of intelligent mines could make their use even more restricted, although the oceans remain enormous areas in which to seek refuge. In weapons, the use of directed energy will increase but is unlikely to change the nature of naval warfare. The speed of processing will make terminal defences more effective, but the offence can counter. New materials will ease the manufacturing processes for ships, but the costs will not decline significantly.

In summary, there seems little prospect for achieving control of the sea in the traditional way. Technologies bring incremental advantages to offence and defence, and only in the field of anti-submarine warfare is there the threat of technological surprise. This suggests military investment in anti-satellite systems would be worthwhile.

CHAPTER 14

The Land–Air Battle

IF THE WAR at sea seems to have evolved into a stately dance of measure and countermeasure, the land war remains potentially as chaotic as ever. History would support those who advocate the overriding importance of the land war. Wars have from time immemorial begun as a result of territorial disputes; the victor in any war is he who gains, or in more recent times does not lose, territory. Control of territory is achieved by occupation. There was a time between the two World Wars that the followers of Douhet believed that wars could be won from the air: that the destruction of an enemy's cities would destroy morale, and hence cause him to surrender. This was proved to be an over simple assumption in World War II. Douhet's successors in the early years of nuclear weapons had similar arguments, which time has also proven simplistic. Land warfare will be necessary at all levels of conflict, as the final arbiter of victory or defeat.

We saw in the first part of the book how land warfare developed through increase in firepower over increasing ranges and it is in these areas that technology will have most to offer the soldier of the future. In defence, protection and mobility, coupled with a capability to disrupt and destroy the enemy advance will be the key. The land battle will take place on the ground, in the air and beyond the atmosphere.

Looking first at the offensive capability, we will examine potentially profitable areas for development. The tank brought a new power and mobility to the battlefield in this century. As a result much thought has subsequently been given to countering the tank. A range of anti-tank weapons has evolved from hand-held launcher, through tank main armament, to air-launched missiles. It is sometimes argued that the day of the tank is coming to an end. For this argument to be sustained, a realistic alternative for advancing and holding territory must be suggested. We shall consider some possibilities.

The tank has three main characteristics: firepower, mobility and protection. These are not independent of each other, as the designer must trade off each against the other to reach his optimum design. Different nations have evolved different philosophies in tank design: some lightly armoured but highly mobile, others with heavy firepower

111

and protection but more lumbering in operation. New material technology is allowing armour to be produced with specific strength and weight characteristics. It may, therefore, be that the tank of the future can be well protected and yet not so heavy as to suffer mobility problems. Certainly advances in composite materials are already providing new levels of protection for armoured vehicles. On the firepower side, work on chemical propellants and warhead design can make some advance in range and penetration power of main armament. Laser sights provide the accuracy. In terms of significant range improvements, the tank will always be limited by its role. It is a direct-fire weapon system fired from a very low altitude, and this will limit its useful range to a few thousand metres, which will continue to be reduced by terrain and other obscuration. The fitting of surface-to-surface missiles is one means to improve range. Purists would no longer call such an armoured vehicle a tank, as for greater range it becomes an indirect fire weapon, or artillery piece. We shall gloss over such distinctions, as the land battle may be fought with a multitude of systems stretching from the individual soldier's bayonet through to the intercontinental strategic missile. The main question is what sort of mix of weapon systems will the developing technologies offer.

Direct-fire weapons have always been a crucial element of the land battle. While longer range weapons can disrupt the enemy, and reduce his ability to reinforce the battle, it is argued that the contact battle is where the war is taking place. Territory is won and lost according to the position of the Forward Edge of the Battle Area (FEBA). This is true at the tactical level, but is not always true at the strategic level. A war consists of many battles and many FEBAs—not a continuous line across the map. Yet it is impossible to imagine a major land war in which the contact battle will not play an essential part. (War against terrorists and insurgents may have a less well-defined line.) If the contact battle is to remain, then the need for direct-fire weapons will also remain. At the shortest ranges the soldier's personal weapon will be needed. It might seem possible that this would be a good opportunity to move from the rifle or machine gun to the directed-energy weapon. The target is normally in line of sight, and at comparatively short range. The limitation of the conventional infantry weapon is the weight of ammunition, and the accuracy of delivery. The directed-energy weapon would need some power source—either chemical fuel or stored electrical energy—and as yet these are likely to be as heavy as the ammunition pouches that could be given up. As developments in sensors and computers continue, it might just become possible to provide bullets with some limited form of terminal guidance: homing either on body heat or the shape of a soldier. The technology would have to provide this at very low cost; otherwise the more cost-effective solution would be simply more ammunition.

The advanced sensors and intelligent warheads become more cost-effective at the level of the hand-held anti-tank weapon system. Current generation weapons are comparatively short range, and leave the user vulnerable to retaliatory fire. The advantages of extending the range are considerable, and development may favour a weapon which can be used in either a direct or indirect fire manner. When enemy tanks are known to be in a particular area, though not in sight, the soldier would elevate the launcher and each warhead would seek its target after launch. This in many ways extends the capability of the dumb mortar into a system which has a hard-kill capability.

The hybrid direct and indirect fire weapon has many advantages in reducing the numbers of different types of equipment, and flexibility in employment. However, its costs are likely to be greater than the sum of its capabilities. Purely indirect-fire weapon systems will continue to play a vital part in the land battle. Artillery has proved itself a battle-winning element in the past, and accurate heavy bombardment will remain an essential element in the future. The key to effective use of artillery is the killing power of the delivered weapons. In the past this has been achieved through larger warheads, greater numbers of guns, faster rates of fire and improvements in delivery accuracy. New technologies can contribute to each of these areas, but some aspects are worth greater investment than others.

The key to the effective use of indirect-fire weapon systems is accuracy. The damage radius of conventional explosive shells is relatively small, and protection against all but direct hits is relatively easy. To achieve high accuracy requires accurate target location information, accurate projectile delivery and feedback of results to allow re-engagement if necessary. While this has been difficult to achieve, the alternative approach of mass of fire delivered to compensate has been adopted. Target location can be achieved through a number of different means. Since the days of the balloon artillery spotter, the advantages of aerial systems has been recognized. As air defence systems have become more difficult to penetrate, the role of the airborne observer has become more hazardous. Two approaches to this problem are possible. One is to develop sensor technologies that allow the reconnaissance platform to operate at a safe distance; the other is to increase the survivability of the reconnaissance systems operating over the battlefield. The reconnaissance sensors may be radar, infrared or visible light, or a combination. The platforms may be high-flying at considerable distances, or low level closer in. Satellite systems will increase in capability to detect concentrations of enemy targets, but will require considerable development on the communications side if they are to provide this information quickly enough.

Drones are replacing manned aircraft for overflight of enemy targets. They can be produced more cheaply and, being smaller, can be made less obvious to enemy air defence systems. However, they are relatively easy targets, and are likely to become increasingly so. It would therefore be unwise to make future indirect-fire weapon systems exclusively dependent on reconnaissance systems which need to overfly enemy-held ground. In the past a range of other target acquisition systems have been developed. Artillery will often be used against headquarters and logistics areas, where the detection of radio emissions can be used for direction finding. When used against enemy artillery, radar can be used to calculate the point of launch of a projectile, or sound direction-finding systems can give positional information. These systems will all have a part to play in the future.

It might be that remote sensors could be developed which could be deployed by artillery itself. Small radar, sound or heat sensor systems, which could be scattered by rocket launch or artillery in known possible areas of enemy activity, could be activated to feed back information for targeting. If such remote systems could provide accurate target positions relative to themselves, this would be sufficient to provide offsets for artillery fire. As times of response decrease, as a function of the increased computing power available, it is possible to conceive of an artillery arrangement whereby the first round fired contains a sensor system which deploys over the general target area, dropping slowly by parachute, and relaying fine detail target information for individual fire correction. Each shell would also be fitted with a form of terminal guidance to its target.

The use of terminal guidance for munitions is under development now. The improvements which will become possible, as the ability to process sensor information increases, will include aiming for vulnerable points on targets, and selection of optimum targets. At the same time new opportunities for the development of countermeasures will open up. If the criteria for target acquisition by the terminally-guided munition can be duplicated in electronic and other decoys, then ground systems will be able to use electronic warfare for defensive purposes.

Conventional howitzer artillery shows little potential for development beyond its current ranges of the order of a few tens of kilometres. To achieve greater ranges requires the shell to have its own propulsion system. These are either in the form of air-breathing motors as in cruise missiles, or rocket motors as in ballistic missiles and artillery rockets. In both cases there are cost advantages in moving towards payloads of multiple intelligent sub-munitions. The vehicle then delivers the payload to the target area, and releases the sub-munitions which individually acquire targets. As range increases, the difficulties in reconnaissance and target-area selection increases significantly. It is no use investing in long-range (beyond about 30km) artillery systems without providing an effective surveillance and target acquisition system which operates out to the required range, and one which provides the information quickly enough for it to be of use.

It is possible that technology will offer some alternatives to conventional propellant for the artillery shells. The development work on ballistic missile defence has already taken the physics of the linear induction motor and converted it into the electromagnetic rail gun. It is, therefore, possible that artillery projectiles could use electrical power, rather than chemical energy, to fire the round. This approach is also applicable to direct-fire weapons, where the much higher muzzle velocities may be significant. Other avenues for research might include the use of high-energy lasers to provide the explosive force for the propellant.

The one system which has provided the long-range firepower, as well as concentration of force in the contact battle, has been the aircraft-delivered munition. Current thinking assumes that the role of the aircraft is decreasing in the immediate area of the land battle, as air defence systems become increasingly effective and are concentrated in the combat area. At this stage it is worth reviewing the future contribution that aircraft have to make in the land-air battle.

In support of the land battle, air systems are used for reconnaissance, offensive air support and transport. The air defence battle contributes both directly and indirectly to the land battle but, apart from ground-based air defence systems, this aspect will be considered in the next Chapter. As discussed above, reconnaissance is a vital link in the conduct of land operations. Aircraft are able to carry more comprehensive systems than small drones, and have much greater flexibility in tasking. They are expensive and more vulnerable. This suggests that the trend will be towards greater use of aircraft surveillance and target-acquisition systems at longer ranges and from the relative security of friendly airspace. Reconnaissance in hostile airspace will move to smaller, less vulnerable and less expensive drones or to satellite systems. The development of drones which can be carried by aircraft would have a number of advantages. The drone's profile could be programmed from the aircraft, and it could be taken rapidly to near the required area for release. Such a stand-off capability for reconnaissance would give the speed and range advantages of the aircraft, and the reduced cost and vulnerability of the drone. The drone could communicate data to the aircraft for backward transmission. The combination of accurate navigation systems with improved computer and sensor systems make this a possible combination for the future.

However, it is in the area of offensive air systems that the future seems most uncertain. It is sometimes argued that the future air defence environment will be so hostile that any system operating above the surface of the earth will not survive. Certainly in areas where the target has its own air defence, an approach by the attacking aircraft within range of that defence is increasingly unwise. There are a number of possible approaches to this problem. First, the use of aircraft-delivered weapons could be discounted in some, or all, scenarios. Secondly, the aircraft can be used in sufficient numbers to overwhelm the defences. Thirdly, the aircraft can reduce vulnerability by a variety of active and passive measures. Fourthly, the aircraft weapons can be designed to be released at a safe distance from the target. Fifthly, the nature of the air system can be changed to improve effectiveness.

Looking at each of these options in turn, we first consider the possibility of a future land battle without aircraft-offensive weapons contributing. For this to be a conceivable option, some alternative method of concentrating firepower would be required. Current aircraft can concentrate in a single attack some five tons or more of conventional high explosive with a high degree of accuracy into a very small area. An attack by a wave of twenty aircraft can deliver 100 tons into a square kilometre with precision, in under five minutes. Comparing this intensity of firepower with artillery illustrates the quite different nature of offensive air attack. With an artillery shell containing around 100lbs of explosive, it takes 200 guns to deliver firepower of equivalent concentration. Those guns are then vulnerable to counter battery fire, and must move. The rapidity of response, coupled with the concentration of firepower, and the radius of action make the offensive aircraft an essential part of the land battle. The more mobile the battle of the future, the more important the contribution that offensive air support can make. It seems likely therefore that weapons delivered from aircraft will have an important part to play in future land battles.

The second option considered was the use of aircraft in sufficient numbers to ensure success. While numbers will always remain an important part of the overall capability of any fighting unit, the cost of aircraft systems as compared with air defence systems is unlikely to make this a sensible route for the future. More important will be investment in reducing vulnerability to air defences, although this will inevitably raise the cost of the aircraft, and reduce the number that can be procured. The techniques for improving survivability will be considered further in the next Chapter, but it is unlikely that the balance between offensive aircraft and air defence systems will move in favour of the aircraft near the FEBA.

This leads inevitably towards the development of weapons which can be released from less hostile airspace and travel under their own power to the target area. The difficulties in moving towards this type of system for land warfare are sometimes understated. The problem of target discrimination, particularly in the immediate area of the contact battle, is very great. It might be that some form of cheap small identification system will have to be provided for friendly force vehicles. Given the difficulties in producing such a reliable system for the much less numerous aircraft, this avenue may not be productive. The use of sensors feeding to pre-stored data in the missile or aircraft computer system is also potentially useful. It does, however, open up the prospect of tailoring decoy systems to spoof such intelligent munitions. Another aspect of the stand-off weapon system is the requirement for target location information. While final terminal guidance may be possible, the missile must place the sub-munitions within a reasonably short distance of the final target set. Long-range artillery has the same problem, and the solution would follow similar surveillance and reconnaissance methods. Indeed, one would expect the ground and air offensive systems to share a common data-gathering system.

The final consideration for future offensive air support is whether technology can provide an alternative platform system to the conventional aircraft. Moves have been made towards greater use for helicopters in this role. Their advantages stem from the ability to use terrain-masking to reduce vulnerability, and increase the time available for target acquisition. The requirement for a large rotating blade assembly makes them less robust than other aircraft. There is also little doubt that the blades would offer a ready avenue for the development of intelligent air defence munitions. The doppler shift associated with the moving blades should be readily identifiable, and might offer an area for early research. What is needed is a weapon platform with the advantageous flight characteristics of a helicopter, but without the inherent fragility. Some would argue that this is found in the Vertical Take-Off and Landing (VTOL) aircraft, although it has not up to now been exploited in that way. The VTOL characteristics are used to allow operations away from airfields but in attack it is used as any other high-performance fixed-wing aircraft. What would be useful would be a robust vehicle able to cross all types of obstruction and terrain, and able to bring fire to bear from heights of up to about 25ft. The hovercraft and the airship fulfil some of these requirements, yet are still extremely fragile. It would seem that until technology provides a more efficient way of overcoming the effects of gravity, con-

TT—I

ventional delivery platforms will remain compromises between vulnerability and effectiveness.

The use of surface-to-surface missiles to replace the aircraft delivery systems is often suggested as the only way forward. The ballistic missile certainly reduces the vulnerability of the offensive air support to air defence. However, there are a number of problems associated with such an approach. The target acquisition system would have to be at least as complex as that of an aircraft and, given the much higher approach speeds, probably more so. If it is to release submunitions, they need time to acquire their targets, which presents a difficult problem in the transition from very high terminal speed ballistic missile carrier to slow speed terminal munitions. The missile is, by its nature, a one-shot system but is likely to have associated costs of similar magnitude to the reusable aircraft platform. There are in addition arms control difficulties associated with ballistic missiles which might make it unwise to become overly dependent on them. If ballistic missiles have problems, then what of the cruise missile? Indeed, having seen an increased role for the drone in reconnaissance, there are attractions to providing the drone itself with the offensive capability, either integrally or through an associated drone. This approach may become increasingly possible as the computing power available increases. It may be that to ensure rapid deployment of such systems to the required area, they will be carried on aircraft. The stand-off weapon then merges into the drone and the offensive cruise missile.

In all these areas the development of more powerful computing capability, small enough to be contained within the weapon, is crucial. At the same time the reconnaissance, surveillance and targeting capability is the key to success, and merits the highest priority for research.

The third area in which air power contributes directly to the land battle is in transport. The logistic supply chain is vital to the army's ability to continue the fight. In the past, improvements to transport brought both strategic and tactical advantages. While sea and motor transport have a continuing and important part to play, given the quantities of logistic support necessary for a modern war, air transport offers the army commander much greater flexibility. That transport is generally provided today by fixed-wing aircraft or helicopters. Hovercraft have found use with the Soviet military, and from time to time there are advocates for the use of airships.

When looking at an army's need for air transport, a number of different requirements exist. At the strategic level, long-range transport is needed for rapid reinforcement overseas. Within a theatre of operations much shorter-range transport is needed to carry out redeployment and resupply. Transport may also be required for rapid movements of forces as the battle dictates. The type of aircraft may be different in each case. For the long-range strategic operations, the essential is large capacity and high speed. The decreasing payload possible in the supersonic region has tended to limit such operations to high subsonic speeds. It seems unlikely that supersonic or ballistic air transport will be a sensible option for strategic air transport within the foreseeable future. Developments are possible in range and capacity, but they will be driven by the requirements for civil air travel in almost all respects. The use of air-to-air refuelling has remained a military activity for extending range, and will continue to be so.

Air transport has also had a role to play in the tactical battle. Within the theatre the helicopter has grown in usefulness for providing the logistic forward supply line. Its ability to ignore the obstacles—natural, man-made or military—between the rear area and the battle zone make it a much more flexible transport system than one tied to ground transport. Speeds limited to less than 200 knots have not been a major drawback, and vulnerability can be reduced by keeping operations sufficiently far back from the contact battle. The key areas for improvement for these logistic support helicopters must be in payload, reliability and reduction in support requirements. Ideally such a supply chain should operate with the helicopter in the air for as great a proportion of the time as possible. Time taken in loading, unloading and refuelling makes the helicopter vulnerable, and reduces the number of missions that can be carried out. Similarly, the larger the payload which can be carried, the more efficient is the resupply chain.

Finally in considering air transport in support of the land battle, its use for mobile operations must be assessed. Troops can be delivered into battle either by parachute drop or by helicopter landing. In either case, they will need time to form up before advancing into contact with the enemy. While this aspect of airborne operations excites considerable interest, it suffers from a number of limitations. If such a force is used as a reserve, then the valuable transport aircraft will have to be put in reserve and their logistic capability is lost. When such a force is put into battle, it will need back-up support by more conventional means, as it will inevitably be more lightly scaled. If the capability is required by nations, it will need considerable investment in dedicated resources. Delivery will tend to favour heliborne troops in future.

This brings us to the wider question of how technology will affect the role of the infantry. There are those who would suggest that the soldier has a declining role to play in the land battle of the future. As technology has taken away the advantages of darkness, provides more reliable ways to detect and kill the soldier, and the firepower of artillery, tanks and aircraft is enhanced, the role of the soldier is too easily forgotten. An important element of land warfare of the future is the quite different environment that has been produced by increasing urbanization. Impressive as the sight of a tank may be in the main street of a modern city, securing the area building by building remains a labour-intensive occupation. Similarly, the traditional roles of the infantry have not been replaced by the greater capability of weapons systems; they have in many cases been enhanced. The automated battlefield, in the sense of robot soldiers slogging it out without human intervention, will remain in the realms of fiction until computer technology offers power comparable to the human brain at the cost of a soldier. This is not a likely near term prospect.

However, the combination of soldier with highly capable man-portable weapons can be effective. provided that the weapon can be produced in sufficient quantity, infantry can provide a significant threat to both armour and aircraft. The development of such air defence weapons is already widespread. The major difficulty in their application in preventing their use against friendly aircraft. What is needed is an identification system which is reliable and simple to interpret. It is possible that improvements in sensors and information-processing could lead to an identification system which could positively identify enemy aircraft to a high degree of confidence. By a simple indicator, or safety interlock, the weapon would then become much more useable on the battlefield. Even this advance would not be easy to provide. The experience of developing such identification systems for major air defence installations suggests that there is a considerable way to go before the small cheap version can be produced.

The problem of the anti-tank weapon is not so great. Identification of the enemy is easier. The developments in such weapons are directed more towards extensions in range, improvements in accuracy and to increasing their ability to penetrate armour. It may be that the use of terminal guidance will have a place here, although it is likely that the advantages of light weight and cheapness will militate against such developments.

In terms of personal weapons, the soldier of the future is portrayed in popular fiction as being armed with a range of capabilities from stun gun to death ray. Directed-energy weapons could be produced as individual systems, but it is doubtful whether it will be worth doing. The advantages would be in accuracy and speed. However the propagation characteristics of laser and particle beam radiation make them more readily countered on the battlefield than elsewhere. The bullet will remain a most effective projectile, with the chemical energy in its charge being an efficient energy-conversion system. The energy requirements for directed-energy weapons are likely to be as cumbersome as the ammunition pouch is today. It is possible that infantry

systems which already require lasers—range-finders and target desig-
nators—could easily be upgraded to have a limited weapon capability,
particularly for use against the eyes of the enemy on the ground or
in the air.

In one respect, technology is making the soldier ever more vulnerable: the increasing potential of chemical weapons, and the hybrids
available through bio-technology. The advances already discussed
may be moving the balance of advantage significantly towards the use
of offensive chemical capability and away from the defensive systems
which have protected troops. If the protective measures necessary to
ensure survival become so encumbering that the infantry lose their
mobility, then it may be that their future fighting options are very
limited. Under such a régime, the close contact battle could only take
place between units encased in heavily-armoured vehicles with integral life support systems. This would bring the complexities and costs
of the aircraft to the provision of ground equipment. This may be
thought an unduly pessimistic outlook for the impact of developments
of biotechnology in chemical, toxin and biological warfare. Yet the
offensive potential is great, and the ability to develop appropriate
defences rapidly is small.

Land warfare has a long history of the use of obstructions, both
natural and manufactured, to hamper the enemy's progress, and put
him in a tactically disadvantageous position. Natural obstacles such as
rivers are improved by the demolition of bridges, and other engineering techniques. New obstacles are made by laying minefields. The
major difficulties with minefields has been the long time that it takes
to lay them, and then the inflexibility of their use. A rapidly-changing
tactical situation can make a friendly obstruction into a major hazard
for friendly troops. Technology offers some relief to both these
problems. The speed of minefield laying can be greatly increased by
laying them from the air, by aircraft, missiles or artillery. The flexibility can be attained by making each mine controllable. The control
could be engineered in a number of different ways. The use of coded
radio signals would give great tactical freedom to the commander, but
is open to many electronic warfare countermeasures. The use of pre-
set timers, giving safe passage times, is a relatively simple and inexpensive innovation, which might offer advantages. At the other end of
the technical scale, an intelligent mine could process the data from its
sensors to determine whether the approaching target was a friendly
or enemy vehicle.

The use of mixed munitions is now developed for aircraft weapon
systems. Anti-airfield weapons use a mix of runway cratering devices,
with mines to deny access to runway repair teams. Current minefields
may mix anti-personnel and anti-armour mines. This could be

extended further in future as intelligent mines become affordable. A mix might include anti-tank mines which seek the vulnerable parts of a tank, mines which home on to radio transmitters, artillery noise, body heat and so on. It is also possible that chemical agents could be released covertly rather than the overt explosion of current mines.

The land-air battle of the future will be as confused and chaotic as that of the past, despite (or perhaps because of) the myriad of new sensor and information-processing techniques. While technology will provide many enhancements to old techniques of land warfare, only the new possibilities of biotechnology offer a step change in the way the land battle is fought. The massive casualties that the machine-gun brought to the infantry in World War I changed the way the land battle was fought, and made the tank battle the key to success. Some would see the helicopter, both as a fighting vehicle and as a troop carrier, changing the nature of future battles in a similar way. Its vulnerability and cost make this unlikely. Only chemical and biological agents offer the cheapness of bullets and a new order of lethality. They will provide the challenge of the future battlefield.

CHAPTER 15

The Aerospace Battle

THE FINAL battle area of the future which we examine is that of warfare above the surface of the earth. We have already seen how the air and space weapon systems are inextricably linked with the war at sea and on the land. War in the future must be a complex mix of systems below, on and above the surface. There is, however, an aerospace battle which is distinct in character from either of the other environments in which air power plays such an important supporting part. Technology has been a major factor in the development of both aircraft and space-weapon systems, and they both depend to a greater extent on technological progress than do surface operations.

The importance of air support to maritime and land operations makes the destruction of enemy air power an important activity. This may take the form of organic air defence systems, which protect the local surface forces, or it may take the form of aerospace warfare against an enemy's ability to use the air for his own purposes. Broadly, countering air power can be done in three ways: preventing enemy air operations, destroying enemy aircraft, or preventing air-delivered weapons from reaching their target.

Current thinking on preventing enemy air operations centres on the design of weapon systems to close airfields. It is a major limitation of aircraft that, for the most part, they rely on a fixed operating base. Conventional modern fixed-wing aircraft need a certain minimum length of fairly smooth runway; they need servicing facilities; they are large consumers of fuel and weapons. These bases cannot be constructed quickly, are easily located and finite in number. They can be attacked by aircraft, missiles or ground troops. They will normally be out of range of conventional artillery. However, there are also significant advantages to the airfield defenders. They can deploy layers of air defence systems, and they can provide hardened protection for the important facilities. They can also switch aircraft about, both locally and between bases. Timing of attacks on airfields is also important. While the closing of an airfield with its aircraft on the ground could be disastrous, if the aircraft are airborne on a mission it may merely be an inconvenience. There are those who foresee the end of the conventional aircraft because of its dependence on the increasingly vulnerable operating base. However, this judgement is premature.

We consider first the likely trends in weapon systems designed to close airfields, and then look at the likely counters. Air-delivered weapons have moved on from the high explosive bomb to the runway penetrator/area denial mix. Current systems require attacking aircraft to come very close to their target before release. Survivability, and hence numbers of successful attacks, would increase if the weapon could be released from a safe distance, and this stand-off capability is achievable with current technology. That said, it is not cheap, and has been long in coming to fruition.

An alternative option for the future which could be considered is to use a surface-to-surface missile rather than an air-to-ground missile. The target is well defined, and would therefore seem particularly well suited to such an approach. There are a number of drawbacks. The hardness of the target means that a considerable weight of munitions must be delivered. Whether it is an air-breathing cruise or a ballistic missile, this increases the size and cost considerably. There are problems of lack of flexibility. The procurement time of such a weapon system might be over ten years, and would then be constrained to a particular tactical situation. Aircraft can have their range extended many times by air-to-air refuelling. Missile range is built in from the start, and can only be altered with considerable re-engineering. Finally, there is a particular difficulty with ballistic missiles in the current strategic arrangement. Decisions about the possibility of their carrying nuclear warheads have to be made quickly, and the danger of mistaken escalation could limit their usefulness. None of this debars nations from going down the route of surface-to-surface missiles designed to close airfields, and the option will be considered when looking at counters.

If most technological effort goes towards providing affordable stand-off air-to-surface weapons, there are possibilities for improving the munitions. The destruction of the runway does not destroy enemy aircraft: it delays their operations. The aircraft will normally be housed in some form of reinforced shelter, and will be controlled from some centralized authority on the base. The fuel and weapons will also be stored in hardened areas. The aircrew and groundcrew will be protected either close to, or with, the aircraft. The targeting of any of these links in the air power chain could pay great dividends. Chemical weapons offer considerable attractions in this respect. Already considerable defensive measures are taken on airfields against chemical attack because they represent particularly suitable targets: geographically well-defined, remote from friendly forces, dependent on highly-skilled irreplaceable manpower. It may be that the mix of munitions for airfield attack would include chemical agents in the future. At one stage further in technological development, the munition dispenser would match its stored information about airfield topography with its sensors, and target individual target-specific munitions on fuel dumps, ammunition stores, operations centres, aircraft hangars and crew quarters. This would be a difficult task to achieve but it is one which, given current sensor and computing capabilities, is theoretically possible.

What counters to airfield vulnerability are in prospect? There are many complementary approaches which will improve the effectiveness of a nation's air power. If the fixed airfield is required, then it can be given many more operating surfaces. The attacking effort required rises very steeply as the number of cuts needed in runways is increased. Emergency runways can be constructed from taxiways and nearby roads. Runways can be widened, and lengthened. It is ironic that a key component of airfield survivability against the high technology offensive may be the comparatively low technology solution of more concrete. Materials technology can also make the concrete more resistant to penetration weapons. Such measures require active air defence as well, to ensure that attacks become too costly to achieve the aim of closing the airfield to operations for a given time. Dispersal of aircraft to other airfields is also a possibility. This will become decreasingly effective as new surveillance systems give rapid information on locations and movements of aircraft. Dispersal into the air, supported by air-to-air refuelling remains an effective, if short-term, countermeasure. Again surveillance with rapid tasking of offensive aircraft may make this a riskier tactic in the future.

The reduction of operating surface requirements for aircraft will make closing runways a considerably more difficult problem. The VTOL aircraft can operate without any runway at all, and away from main bases. That said, it pays a design penalty in the form of payload and range. It still requires the logistics support of normal aircraft and, if operating away from main bases, lacks hardened protection. Many of the advantages of VTOL can be enjoyed by reducing the landing and take-off distances. For conventional fixed-wing flight, the limiting distance for runway length in future is likely to be the required landing run. Portable automatic microwave landing systems could be developed, which would be placed at the touchdown point on a damaged runway, to give a safe landing. The attack requirements to close the runway would then rise to a level where the effort became unsupportable.

While such techniques could allow aircraft to continue operating from a badly damaged runway, the problem becomes more difficult should their shelters become vulnerable. At this stage of offensive capability, it might become necessary to operate from further back, and make greater use of air-to-air refuelling. This would make it more difficult for enemy aircraft to reach the release point for their anti-airfield weapons and, if geography permitted, the airfields could be far enough back to be beyond the design range of deployed surface-to-surface missiles.

The use of more capable chemical weapons in the future may make it necessary to offer far greater redundancy in airfield operations. Fuel pipelines could be tapped off to convenient roads; weapon stocks could be stored on mobile carriers; command and control could be conducted from airborne headquarters. None of these requirements is beyond current technology; but all are expensive.

For the future, it will remain productive for aircraft to try to prevent the other side's air operations by attacking his airfields, and on the other hand there will remain counters to reduce the effectiveness of such attacks. The second element of the air battle is the destruction of enemy aircraft. We have considered the methods on the ground, and now consider the problem in the air.

Air defence is a complex integration of detection and target identification systems, communication, control, and weapon systems. While the destruction of enemy aircraft is of itself an aim, their destruction before they carry out their mission is much more desirable. As stand-off offensive weapons are developed, this means that the attacking aircraft must be detected, identified and engaged at ever greater ranges. Detection is predominantly done by radar. Radar ranges are, under normal conditions, a maximum of the order of the line of sight distance. Certain atmospheric conditions can extend this, and development work on over-the-horizon systems gives the prospect of extended range. However the easiest way to extend radar ranges is by raising the height of the system: either airborne or satellite. The problem is greater with identification. As air defence missiles of greater range are developed, the need for a positive long-range identification system is even stronger. The advances in electronic warfare have made the current radar transponder system unreliable in war. What is needed is an automatic long-range identification arrangement which is more akin to one person recognizing someone from memory, than a sentry asking a stranger for a password.

How does one person recognize another? Information from the senses is processed by the brain and compared with past experience. In the same way, for future identification information will have to be obtained from every possible sensor, processed by computers and compared with stored criteria. For an aircraft target, radar images gathered by airborne radars—even in hostile electronic conditions—

may be processed to provide information about size and shape as well as location. Satellite infra-red detection might add information about engine and skin temperatures. Sound detectors might be moored at sea, or carried by balloons. Route mapping would indicate departure area, and possible aircraft types and capabilities, and options for missions. All this data would have to be communicated in the hostile electronic warfare environment, processed to arrive at the most probable identification, and then retransmitted to the air defence weapon system. This is not an easy development and will be both costly and technically difficult. Nevertheless, there is little point in developing ever more capable air defence weapons if those capabilities are unusable because the target cannot be identified.

What can be done to hamper this work towards a more reliable air defence identification and target acquisition arrangement? Ideally an attacking aircraft should aim to avoid detection by air defence systems. The simplest way, until the development of airborne radar systems which can discriminate between ground reflections and moving targets, has been to fly at as low a height as possible. This has some disadvantages. The demands on the pilot and aircraft systems are much greater, and target acquisition times are much shorter. The aircraft flies within the lethal range of many ground force air defence systems, both friendly and hostile. Terrain screening will be a decreasingly effective technique as airborne radars become the norm. However, it will still be necessary to fly at low level to make the less expensive, more numerous and more capable ground radars ineffective. Reducing radar cross-section (Stealth), decreasing infra-red emissions and improving means of electronic deception will all be necessary. However, it may be that the new sensors, both airborne and space-based, become so effective that they must become high priority targets themselves. Here one can see technology providing missiles which locate the sensor system by its radar, or data link, radiations.

Again, in the battle between air defence system and attacking aircraft, there is no end to the measure and countermeasure development. Nor is there an apparent cost advantage to offence or defence in the current technological battle: both are so expensive as to prevent complete deployment. This means that missiles and bombs will be released, and the final line of defence will be to destroy the incoming warhead before it reaches its target. At first sight the problem of destroying the relatively small and high velocity incoming munition, in the relatively short time between release and impact, seems far more difficult than destroying the weapon carrier.

However, the defence does have a number of advantages. Whether it is a ship, an aircraft or a land target, it will be a well-defined and finite area which has to be defended. The incoming warhead will be open to attack at decreasing ranges, so that acquisition and aiming become progressively easier (as success becomes progressively more important). While complex anti-missile missiles will be needed for engagement at long distances, high velocity multibarrel gun fire may be effective at close range. At close ranges directed-energy weapons may have a role to play. The power requirements will be more easily met on a ship or on land. The speed of response is important, and at the shorter ranges propagation should not be a problem. It could be that such weapons would be laser in the near term, with the possibility of microwave radiation in the medium term, and possibly particle beam in the longer term. There may also be a role for the electromagnetic rail gun technology in this form of terminal defence. The ability to accelerate material to very high velocities could be used like a shot gun against incoming weapons. Such systems will not provide a total answer in every case. They will be expensive, and will have a limited arc of engagement. This means that as offensive missiles are programmed to attack from any direction, all-round cover will be needed. Missiles which split into a mix of decoys and warheads will further confuse the defence. Yet again there will be a technological battle between defence and offence. However, in this case it appears likely that investment in terminal protection of the most important targets, such as command and control centres, nuclear systems, centres of government, airborne radars, ports and communications, may prove worthwhile.

Other air power contributions for the future, such as reconnaissance, close air support, interdiction and maritime operations were discussed in the preceding two Chapters. One element not covered was the use of air power for strategic forces. We saw in Chapter 4 how the use of the bomber developed, particularly with the advent of nuclear weapons, into an instrument of strategic warfare. The place of the manned aircraft has declined in recent times as the strategic ballistic missile has offered greater assurance of the nuclear warhead reaching its target. This may not be the case in the future. The entirely reasonable desire among nations to reduce the number of nuclear weapons has led to a series of arms control agreements. These naturally centre on those systems where verification is most easily enforced. The unambiguous nature of a long-range missile makes it an attractive category of weapon for arms treaties. These treaties will not eliminate (nor in today's world would it be desirable for them to do so) the nuclear weapon. It is, however, more likely that strategic forces will be provided by a higher proportion of aircraft. For nuclear deterrence to remain credible, there must be a reasonable degree of assurance that these weapons could reach their targets. The technologies involved will be no different from those already discussed to improve aircraft survivability: low level transit, electronic warfare, stealth, suppression of enemy air defences and stand-off weapons. The importance of this area to states with strategic nuclear forces is such that improving the capability of offensive aircraft is likely to be a preferred option to wholesale replacement by unmanned systems.

Ballistic and cruise missiles are unlikely to disappear entirely through arms control. While the SALT agreements put limits on numbers, and the INF agreement has reduced the number of intermediate-range weapons, the nuclear powers, and perhaps a gradually increasing number of other states, will wish to field at least a minimal missile-based nuclear force. Developments will be directed towards improving pre-launch survivability, reducing in-flight vulnerability and increasing reliability. There is not much further improvement to be made on accuracy or range. The pre-launch survivability has been sought in the past through different basing methods, increased numbers and mobility. Arms limitations have tended to constrain the options available. As the retention of an assured retaliatory capability, even following a surprise attack, is so important to the stability of nuclear deterrence, care will be needed to ensure that future arms control agreements do not adversely affect this aspect.

For submarine-based ballistic missiles, submarine design and tactical doctrine are the key areas. For land-based missiles, there are no easy answers. Mobility will help make the counter-force targeting problem more difficult, but also compounds command and control problems and vulnerabilities. Deep silos with multiple exits offer another route, but one which is not inexpensive. Trading multiple warheads for an equivalent number of single warhead missiles is another possibility. However, at the current numbers of strategic systems, a pre-emptive disabling attack is not feasible. The problem will only become acute if the numbers of nuclear missiles decrease markedly, at which stage extra investment will become necessary in those remaining.

The continuing work on defensive measures against strategic missiles, discussed in Chapter 8, means that complementary work on improving in-flight survivability will be needed. Fortunately, this is a considerably simpler technical problem than the deployment of a functional strategic defence system. Counters to space-based attacks during the boost-phase could include reduction in boost phase times. Missiles would be accelerated more quickly so that the time spent in the relatively more vulnerable powered phase was reduced, and the acquisition, targeting and destruction cycle time required became impossibly short. The use of decoys, ablative materials or spin to dissipate energy from lasers and low trajectory are all likely. The defence during the terminal phase would draw on similar technologies to the terminal air defence developments considered earlier. This could prove reasonably successful in the defence of point targets, such as missile silos, but would not be feasible for large area targets.

In the strategic nuclear arrangements, the most important consideration is that of command and control. The authorization for the use of such weapons must be retained at the level of Head of State, but the system must be able to respond to such authorization under all conditions. It is crucial, therefore, that the major investment is made in the security and reliability of the command system, both to ensure that unauthorized release of nuclear weapons is not possible, and also that the arrangements for properly authorized release are credible. There would be much to be said for the incorporation of a ground-controlled disabling device in all strategic missiles, so that weapons could be rendered harmless at any point up to impact, given the right code. This would provide extra insurance against any form of accidental launch. Certainly the technology for Permissive Action Links (warhead locking control system) should be made available to all new nuclear powers, to ensure control of weapons is retained at the highest level.

The requirements for a reliable command, control and communication system for strategic nuclear forces is a demanding one. Dependence on vulnerable communication systems must be avoided. Satellites would be vulnerable to an exo-atmospheric nuclear explosion, particularly from the effect of the nuclear electromagnetic pulse. Ground radio communications would also suffer from both destruction of equipment and nuclear effects on propagation. The use of fibre-optic lines buried deep, and with redundancy of routing, would offer one option. Whatever is done towards protecting the integrity of the system will not be cheap.

The aerospace battle will take place over land, over the sea, in the air, in the upper reaches of the atmosphere, and finally in space. In one sense, military use of space is merely an extension of the ancient desire for control of the high ground. It is true that satellites in orbit provide coverage of vast areas of the earth's surface. Technology is providing ever more discriminating sensors to overcome the disadvantages of distance, so that space-based reconnaissance can have tactical influences. More and more the clarity and range of satellite communications systems are being employed down to the battlefield level. Orbiting stations will provide three-dimensional positioning information to military units on the land, at sea and in the air.

Future wars are seen as being fought with a quite extraordinary dependence on space-based systems. The commander tasks an offensive air mission on the basis of satellite reconnaissance data, communicated by satellite relay, to an aircraft which is navigated by satellite position information, with a tactical display relayed by communications satellite, and releases a missile which uses the same navigational system, with the post-attack reconnaissance gathered directly or indirectly through yet another satellite. Putting aside the cost of fielding such a system universally, it gives rise to considerable concerns about future vulnerabilities. As was discussed in Chapter 3, the greatest military advantage may come from the deployment of an effective anti-satellite capability. The use of missiles, which can be ground-based, air-launched or space-based is within current technological ability. The counters that are possible are significantly more expensive. It is true that using high earth orbits makes the destruction of satellites much more difficult, but it also degrades the performance of the satellite system. In this potential battle for measure and counter-measure in space, it may be that the victory will go to the side which can operate without space-based systems, while at the same time denying the use of space to the opposition.

If this is the case, then the strategy to be adopted would require the development of an effective form of anti-satellite capability, a return to lower altitude methods of surveillance, targeting, communications and navigational assistance. For those areas where space-based systems offer great enough benefits, it might be worth investing in a short notice launch capability to replace destroyed satellites. Alternatively, low orbital missiles could deploy short-lived systems. This would be an expensive option. Anti-satellite weapons could become subject to arms control, given the importance of early warning systems to strategic stability. This would not affect the general need to reduce dependence on space-based systems. The covert development of anti-satellite weapons would be possible. In any event, the use of exo-atmospheric nuclear weapons would be an effective method of putting satellites out of commission.

If the passive military systems in space are becoming more vulnerable, what of the basing of offensive systems outside of the atmosphere? Since the costs of developing such systems, and then deploying them in space, would be far greater than giving similar destructive capabilities to long-range weapon systems—missile, aircraft/missile, ship/missile—this seems an unproductive use of resources. Such systems would have the same vulnerability problems as the passive satellites, and defensive systems would increase their costs yet further. Only when there is no other way of carrying out an operation should space-based weapons be considered. This will be when the time of response is critical, and is why space-based systems have been considered for countering strategic nuclear missiles. The inherent limitations of such a system were covered in Chapter 8.

Beyond the immediate orbit of the earth, there are few possibilities for the use of space to affect military operations on the planet. Military installations on the moon would cost more to run than orbiting systems and would suffer from the same vulnerabilities. It might, however, be worth using the moon itself as an indestructible reflector in the sky for communications purposes. It could in time, if civilian manned exploration of the moon becomes economically worthwhile, be possible to provide a large number of hardened relay stations to improve this capability.

The aerospace battle of the future does not offer the prospect of ever higher and ever faster weapon systems. The short period when the skies and beyond were relatively free areas for military operations is over. Aerospace power will continue to be critical in the exercise of military strength, but at best it is likely to be centred on denying its use to an enemy. For offensive aircraft, counters to air defences and stand-off missiles will need continual development. Alternatives to satellite systems will be essential, as will a capability to destroy the enemy's satellites. If some success can be achieved in this, then investment in the expensive space-based systems can be reduced.

CHAPTER 16

Science and the Military Tomorrow

HISTORY has shown us many examples of the critical role that technology has played in military capability. There were many more examples, not covered in this volume, of hopes for technical breakthroughs which were discarded because they proved too expensive, ineffective or impossible to develop. The promise of atomic power did not make the atomic aircraft a workable military development. The development of modern jet aircraft was not a story of unbroken successes. Much money was spent on designs, such as the ill-fated TSR2, which were never to provide any defence capability. Similar problems have dogged the development of rocket systems. In Britain, the Blue Streak missile was cancelled because of costs and concerns about vulnerability. In the United States, high technology weapons systems, such as air defence guns, have been cancelled late in development in recent years for reasons of cost, lack of reliability and inability to carry out the task.

Even when technology provides a new defence capability, it may be years before it is tested in combat, and it may then be found wanting. The shooting down of a civil airliner in the Gulf by the Vincennes in 1988 caused many to question the relevance of the most modern radar and command system in the world, if it remained possible to shoot down a civil airliner in the belief that it was a hostile fighter. The revelations in the aftermath of the Space Shuttle disaster showed how dependent high technology is on the reliability of the multitude of subsystems. The Chernobyl disaster demonstrated that technological failure, whether through human or system error, knows no international boundaries, and respects no expert opinion.

What then should our strategy for research and development be? While nations are threatened, either from inside or without, they must be prepared for the developing capabilities of their potential enemies. The research that they undertake on new weapon systems may make them more, rather than less, vulnerable. The new weapon system may be technically flawed, and the resources spent on it could have produced more effective defence if invested elsewhere. The new system may work perfectly, but yet still be flawed in concept. An increasing dependence on a highly capable technical device makes for a greater vulnerability to effective counter-measures. Finally, when the potential enemy develops his own version of the new technology—as he surely will—security may be less than it was before either side had the new capability.

What is needed is a certain way of deciding which technologies will improve future security. If the history of war shows nothing else, it demonstrates that such a certainty is impossible. In our review of past successes, many depended on the lucky coincidence of the technologies and a single-minded enthusiast. It often appears that those times are past, and that new scientific discoveries depend on vast research teams working in expensive facilities for contract production. That such an approach can produce results is not in doubt, but it still depends on the original thoughts of the team members. The Manhattan Project was a perfect example of what it is possible to achieve with great resources, the finest brains, and a single objective. The question is whether the organization for military research allows innovative thinking, and having had a potentially useful idea is capable of following it up, and developing an affordable effective weapon system.

It is not the intention of the author to list the changes necessary to the differing organizations already in being in the many defence establishments throughout the world. Each nation has different security concerns, resource constraints, scientific base and industrial capability. Rather we can draw a few indicators from the past as to possible approaches for the future.

Firstly, it is clear that pure scientific research is the key to both commercial and military technology. In many cases, interesting scientific novelties are turned into commercial products, which in turn lead to military capabilities. The laser is a recent example. Without the stage of pure non-applied research, radical innovation is unlikely. To achieve a breakthrough in such pure research areas has in general required free interchange of information between academic institutions. The nature of academic research is such that it thrives on debate and criticism. Such open discussion and publication often appear against the interests of the military applications. Nevertheless, the best research will come from unfettered academic institutions, and it will be a matter of debate to what extent military funding is compatible with generating ideas which will be of equal use to potential enemies.

Whatever the source of funds, there is no doubt that the potential military applications of new discoveries must be a key interest to the defence establishment. It is therefore necessary to have expert opinion available which can spot potential applications at an early stage. Such groups exist in military research establishments, but may for entirely rational reasons have a narrow view of the future military requirement. In some way, it is necessary to harness the imagination of the scientist engineer in the service of national defence needs. This is a particularly difficult arrangement to put in place. Ideally the defence policy makers should have a good scientific background, but in practice few, whether politician, military or government official, are likely to be so qualified. While scientific specialists can be engaged, they will be likely to respond to the direction given by the non-specialist leaders. The tank and the aircraft both suffered from the lack of vision of officialdom. Perhaps the defence industries and the government should seek to fund university departments in Weapon Technology, where researchers would be given freedom to choose their own avenues of research. The Strategic Studies centres of the world are almost all the off-spring of history, social science or other humanities departments.

While such centres of research effort might improve the chances of utilizing new technologies to enhance security, they would not prevent the mistakes of the past. Indeed it could be argued that such centres would form yet one more lobby group for expensive new weapon systems. While this might be a danger, it could be overcome given sufficient numbers of independent research projects. The difficulty would be where funds were tied to particular objectives. The experience of research for the Strategic Defence Initiative showed how such directed activity can keep the momentum of projects going independently of the strategic rationale. A big spending complex activity can become a gravy train for all, and it becomes difficult to halt.

A different approach to the problem of increasing costs for new technologies could be to accept second place in the race for innovation. This option will not appeal to defence industries or the military, but it has a number of advantages for both. The key concern for the future is the increasing costs of weapon systems with finite resources available. This leads to the classic road to absurdity where eventually the whole of a nation's defence budget must go on a single new aircraft. Looking at the high technology in the civilian sector, the research and pricing strategy of computer firms may have some lessons to offer. The expensive computers are those on the frontiers of the possible. As chip densities increase, parallel processing becomes available, speeds rise, and display systems improve a new and better system is launched. The new system may be incompatible with those that have gone before which raises the cost yet further. The cheaper models come from those producers prepared to stay behind the front runners. They use mature technologies where production costs have dropped and software is fully developed. It can be that the advantages of reliable mature technologies at less cost outweigh the promise of new better systems which lack support.

If all nations adopted such a wait and see approach then new weapons would not be developed. Unlikely as this may seem now, it may become increasingly possible in the future as cost and resource constraints affect even the Superpowers. It may be that the current flurry of activity in arms control is the first indication of such a new approach. If the current optimism on arms reductions is carried through to significant decreases in levels of armament, then there will be much less enthusiasm for new weapon technologies. While such moves can improve stability between the Superpowers, it will not affect the risks that modern weapons in the hands of less stable regimes present. Indeed it is already clear that technology is offering considerable capabilities to those involved in low intensity conflict around the world. It may be that the high technology nations will need to direct more effort to the prevention of the spread of the more damaging developments. Biotechnology is but one area where proliferation of production techniques for chemical, toxin and biological agents could be very dangerous.

Perhaps the only answer to the effective application of science in the service of the military is as broad an education as possible for all concerned in developing weapons. The scientist needs to be aware of what he is doing in the strategic context, if he is to spot the innovations which are worth developing. The policymaker must be able to make intelligent judgements on the relative merits of different technologies, and for this needs both basic scientific and statistical grounding. The organization must be sufficiently responsive to correct its procurement strategy when circumstances change. The gambler who keeps doubling his stakes as his losses increase has much in common with the organization which throws ever increasing amounts of money to make some new super technology work. It may be that a new wonder weapon is the eventual result, but many more less capable systems might have been deployed in shorter times. Judging the balance of risk will never be easy, but the options must be continually examined.

This book has produced no easy answer to the technology trap. Success stories seem obvious with the advantage of historical perspective. The failures of the past may yet return as new successes. The interesting effect in the research laboratory, such as high temperature superconductivity, may need years of development and some discovery in an unrelated field before it is transformed into a novel weapon. The military man must remain responsive to new ideas, yet sceptical of magic forecasts. The decision maker must weigh the costs against the benefits, and be prepared to review decisions in the light of developments. The effect of the introduction of new weapons on stability and opportunities for arms control must not be ignored. The changing nature of the threat will mean that high cost weapons should be flexible in application as insurance against an uncertain future. The military and science will continue to be necessary partners until conflict is no longer possible.

Notes

Chapter 2—Maritime Warfare

1. B. & F. M. Brodie, *From Crossbow to H-bomb* (Indiana University Press 1973), p. 162.
2. For arguments which strike many chords with the present day advocacy for technical quality rather than quantity, see 'The Tactical Qualities of the Dreadnought Type of Battleship' by W. S. Sims, in *Brassey's Naval Annual 1907*. This has been reprinted in *From Ironclad to Trident*, edited by B. Ranft (Brassey's 1986), pp. 62–6.
3. Brodie, *op. cit.*, p. 181.
4. For a description of General Mitchell's career see A. F. Hurley, *Billy Mitchell: Crusader for Air Power* (Bloomington 1975).
5. R. Higham, *Air Power* (St Martin's Press, NY 1972), pp. 162–91.
6. During World War I an Allied Submarine Detection Investigation Committee was established. It was not until just after the end of the war that the technique of using ultrasonic echoes for detecting submarines was perfected. However, the equipment took its name ASDIC from the initials of the committee. The term Sonar (Sound Navigation and Ranging) is the modern equivalent.
7. *The Military Balance 1988–89* (IISS 1988).
8. *Ibid.*
9. *Soviet Military Power 1986.* US Department of Defence, p. 29.
10. J. M. Collins, *US-Soviet Military Balance Statistical Trends 1970–1983*, CRS Report 84-163 S, p. 95.
11. C. A. Sorrels, *US Cruise Missile Programs* (Brassey's 1983), inside front cover.
12. *Ibid*, pp. 129–31.
13. *Ibid.*, p. 131.

Chapter 3—Land Warfare

1. F. A. Beer, *Peace against War* (Freeman, San Francisco 1981), p. 45.
2. B. & F. M. Brodie, *From Crossbow to H-bomb* (Indiana University Press 1973), pp. 131–2.
3. *Ibid*, p. 145.
4. H. Strachan, *European Armies and the Conduct of War* (Allen & Unwin, London 1983), pp. 117–18.
5. Brodie, *op. cit.*, p. 196.
6. Strachan, *op. cit.*, p. 143.
7. I. B. Holley, *Ideas and Weapons* (Office of Air Force History, Washington, 1983) p. 18.
8. *Ibid.*, p. 19. Holley reports an assessment that 27.3 per cent of the American Expeditionary Force were from gas.
9. For Liddell Hart's conversion to tanks by Fuller see B. Bond, *Liddell Hart* (Cassell, London 1977), pp. 27–30.
10. A good short description of the evolution and practice of *Blitzkrieg* is in Strachan, *op. cit.*, pp. 150–68.

Chapter 4—Air and Space Warfare

1. B. & F. M. Brodie, *From Crossbow to H-Bomb* (Indiana University Press 1973), pp. 173–5.
2. R. Higham, *Air Power* (St Martin's Press, New York 1972), pp. 21–3.
3. I. B. Holley, *Ideas and Weapons* (Office of Air Force History, Washington 1983), pp. 26–32.
4. G. Douhet, *The Command of the Air*, translated by D. Ferrari and republished by Office of Air Force History, Washington 1983.
5. Higham, *op. cit.*, pp. 41–3.
6. J. Terraine, *Right of the Line* (Hodder & Stoughton, London 1985), p. 22.
7. For the best account of all aspects of the effects of technological developments in World War II see Terraine, *op. cit.*
8. Brodie, *op. cit.*, p. 231.

Chapter 5—High Energy Physics

1. For a review of the current thinking on the nature of matter see 'Elementary Particles and Forces' by C. Quigg, in *Scientific American*, April 1985, pp. 64–75.
2. *Ibid.*, pp. 74–5. Quigg describes a proposed 1 TeV (million million electron volt) accelerator known as the Superconducting Supercollider which could accelerate protons to energies of 20 TeV within a loop some 30 km in diameter. It could be built by 1994 at a cost of $3 billion.
3. 'Fusion Power with Particle Beams' by G. Yonas, in *Scientific American*. November 1978, pp. 40–51. For a discussion on progress in using infra-red laser beams for fusion see 'Progress in Laser Fusion' by R. S. Craxton, R. L. McCrory & J. M. Soures in *Scientific American*, August 1986, pp. 60–71.
4. 'Laser Light' by A. L. Schawlow, in *Scientific American*, September 1968, pp. 120–36.
5. 'Particle Beam Weapons' by J. Parmentola & K. Tsipis, in *Scientific American*, April 1979, pp. 38–49.
6. 'Advances in Antisubmarine Warfare' by J. S. Wit, in *Scientific American*, February 1981, p. 30.
7. 'Laser Weapons' by K. Tsipis, in *Scientific American*, December 1981, pp. 39–40.
8. Report on Ballistic Missile Defence of North Atlantic Assembly Scientific and Technical Committee of November 1983 gives review of options.
9. For a review of the technical capabilities and requirements of laser weapons for ballistic missile defence see 'Strategic Defense and Directed-Energy Weapons' by C. Kumar, N. Patel & N. Bloemberger, in *Scientific American*, September 1987.
10. High power radio frequency weapons can also be produced from non-laser systems using microwave generators. The Soviet Union is reported to have achieved 500 Megawatts at a frequency of 3 GHz. For a report on progress in this area see B. Jasani, 'Space Weapons and International Security', SIPRI, Oxford University Press 1987, pp. 26–7.
11. For a possible system see: 'SDIO Studies basing Small X-Ray Laser Weapons on Submarines' by T. M. Foley in *Aviation Week & Space Technology*, 1 August 1988, pp. 57–64.

Chapter 6—Computing Science

1. *The Penguin Computing Book* by S. Curran and R. Curnow, Penguin, London 1983, p. 83.
2. 'Computers' by S. M. Ulam, in *Scientific American*, September 1964, pp. 203–6.
3. 'The Fundamental Physical Limitations of Computation' by C. H. Bennett & R. Landauer, in *Scientific American*, July 1985, p. 45.
4. Curran & Curnow, *op. cit.*, p. 381.
5. 'Supercomputers' by R. D. Levine, in *Scientific American*, January 1982, pp. 112–24.
6. 'The Connection Machine' by W. D. Hillis, in *Scientific American*, June 1987, pp. 86–93.
7. For a discussion of the approaches to parallel processing see 'Advanced Computer Architectures' by G. C. Fox and P. C. Messina, in *Scientific American*, October 1987.
8. 'The Superconducting Computer' by J. Matisco, in *Scientific American*, May 1980, pp. 38–53.

9. 'Tripping the Light Fantastic', in *Scientific American*, August 1986, pp. 57B–58.
10. 'Collective Computation in Neuronlike Circuits' by D. W. Tank & J. J. Hopfield, in *Scientific American*, December 1987, pp. 62–70.
11. 'Computer Software for Intelligent Systems' by D. B. Lenat, in *Scientific American*, September 1984, pp. 152–60.
12. 'Human Error blamed in Vincennes Report' by D. Harvey, in *Flight International*, 3 September 1988.
13. 'Expert Systems in C^2 Systems' by C. J. Harris, in *Advances in C^3 Systems*, edited by C. J. Harris & I. White (Peregrinus, London 1987), pp. 307–21.
14. 'Los Alamos Carries Research Beyond Physical Boundaries' by W. B. Scott, *Aviation Week & Space Technology*, 25 July 1988, pp. 36–8.

Chapter 7—Nuclear Physics

1. Leo Szilard quoted in *From Crossbow to H-Bomb* by B. & F. M. Brodie (Indiana University Press, 1973), p. 236.
2. 'Enhanced-Radiation Weapons' by F. M. Kaplan, in *Scientific American*, May 1978, pp. 44–51.
3. For a technical description see 'The Effects of Nuclear War' by the Office of Technical Assessment (Croom Helm, London 1980).
4. 'Third Generation Nuclear Weapons' by T. B. Taylor, in *Scientific American*, April 1987, pp. 22–31.
5. Even the potential of laser fusion seems to require enormous supporting equipment. See 'Progress in Laser Fusion' by R. S. Craxton, R. L. McCrory & J. M. Soures, in *Scientific American*, August 1986, pp. 60–71. This paper also gives a good descripion of computer simulation of the nuclear processes.

Chapter 8—Space Technology

1. 'Space: the Military Applications Today and Tomorrow' by T. Garden, in *RUSI & Brassey's Defence Yearbook 1985*, pp. 149–61.
2. 'Advances in Antisubmarine Warfare' by J. S. Wit, in *Scientific American*, February 1981, pp. 27–37.
3. 'Space Science, Space Technology and the Space Station' by J. A. Van Allen, in *Scientific American*, January 1986, p. 29.
4. 'The Development of Command, Control, Communications and Intelligence Systems' by M. van der Veen, in *The Militarisation of Space*, ed. S. Kirby and G. Robson (Wheatsheaf 1987), pp. 13–19.
5. 'Strategic Command and Control and the Militarisation of Space' by M. Clarke, in *ibid.*, pp. 30–6.
6. The difficulties are well described in *Space Weapons and International Security*, ed. B. Jasani (SIPRI 1987), pp. 36–45.
7. A good collection of the various views on SDI is found in *The Strategic Defense Debate*, ed. C. Snyder (Philadelphia 1986).

Chapter 9—Chemistry

1. 'Chemical Warfare: A Primer on Agents, Munitions, and Defensive Measures' by E. M. Kallis, Congressional Research Service Report 81–97F of 27 April 1981.
2. 'Chemical Warfare and Chemical Disarmament' by M. Meselson & J. P. Robinson, in *Scientific American*, April 1980, pp. 34–43.
3. 'Chemical Weapons and the Third World' by G. K. Vachon, *Survival*, March/April 1984, p. 80.
4. *Chemical Weapons and Western Security Policy* by the Aspen Strategy Group (University Press of America, 1988), p. 10, reported that: 'It seems improbable that technological changes per se could put defense at a disadvantage in any decisive way, provided that

Western intelligence is adequate to give warning of new and threatening developments.' This is an overly optimistic assessment in the author's view. A more sobering review of defensive technological capabilities appears in: *Deterring Chemical Warfare: US Policy Options for the 1990's* by H. Stringer (Pergamon, Oxford 1986), pp. 48–9.

Chapter 10—Materials Science

1. 'Materials for Aerospace' by M. A. Steinberg, in *Scientific American*, October 1986, pp. 59–64.
2. For a detailed explanation of the new processing techniques see 'Advanced metals' by B. H. Kear, in *Scientific American*, October 1986, pp. 137–45.
3. 'Composites' by T-W Chou, R. L. McCullough & R. B. Pipes, in *Scientific American*, October 1986, p. 170.
4. Reported in *Scientific American*, December 1987, p. 23.
5. 'Materials for Information and Communication' by J. S. Mayo, in *Scientific American*, October 1986, pp. 51–7.

Chapter 11—Biotechnology

1. For account of historic uses of biological warfare see *Biological and Toxin Weapons Today*, ed. E. Geissler, (SIPRI 1986), pp. 7–13. 'The Birth of the US Biological-Warfare Program' by B. J. Bernstein, in *Scientific American*, June 1987, pp. 94–9, reviews the work done in the United States during World War II.
2. *Biotechnology: A New Industrial Revolution* by S. Prentis (Orbis, London 1985) pp. 36–65.
3. *Guide to Germ Warfare*, TM3–216/AFM 355–6 (Departments of the Army and the Air Force, Washington 1956).
4. Geissler, *op. cit.*, pp. 14–15.
5. Biotechnology processes can also be used to produce chemical warfare agents and toxins. For more details see *Deterring Chemical Warfare: US Policy Options for the 1990's*, by H. Stringer (Pergamon, Oxford 1986), pp. 24–6.
6. Prentis, *op. cit.*, p. 178.

Chapter 12—Electronics

1. 'Extremely Low Frequency Communications System', in *C³I Handbook* (Defense Electronics, California 1986), pp. 86–8.
2. 'Packet Radio: A Survivable Communications System' by B. H. Davies & T. R. Davies, in *Advances in Command, Control & Communications Systems*, ed. C. J. Harris & K. I. White (Peregrinus, London 1987), pp. 159–82.
3. 'Over-the-Horizon Backscatter Radar', in *C³I Handbook, op. cit.*, pp. 99–102.
4. 'Phased-Array Radars' by E. Brookner, in *Scientific American*, February 1985, pp. 76–84.
5. 'The C3 Laser' by W. T. Tsang, in *Scientific American*, November 1984, pp. 126–35.
6. 'Advances in Antisubmarine Warfare' by J. S. Wit, in *Scientific American*, February 1981, p. 30.
7. 'Some Aspects of Data Fusion' by G. B. Wilson, in Harris & White, *op. cit.*, pp. 321–38. Also in the same volume, 'An AI Approach to Data Fusion and Situation Assessment' by W. L. Lakin & J. A. H. Miles, pp. 339–77.
8. 'Data Fusion for C³I Systems', in *C³I Handbook, op. cit.*, pp. 217–26.

Bibliography

C3I Handbook. Defense Electronics, California 1986.
Guide to Germ Warfare. Department of Army & Air Force, Washington 1956.
Soviet Military Power 1986. DOD, Washington 1986.
The Military Balance 1988–89. IISS, London 1988.
Asimov, I. *A Short History of Chemistry*. Heinemann, London 1972.
Aspen Strategy Group. *Chemical Weapons and Western Security*. University Press of America 1987.
Bajusz, W. *Deterrence, Technology and Strategic Arms*. IISS, Adelphi Paper 215, London 1986.
Barnaby, F. *Future War*. Joseph, London 1984.
Beer, F. A. *Peace Against War*. Freeman, San Francisco 1981.
Bennett, C. H. & Landauer, R. The fundamental limitations of computing. *Scientific American*, July 1985.
Bertram, C. (ed.) *New Conventional Weapons and E-W Security*. Macmillan, London 1979.
Bidwell, S. *World War 3*. Prentice Hall, New Jersey 1978.
Bond, B. *Liddel Hart*. Cassel, London 1977.
British Medical Association. *The Medical Effects of Nuclear War*. Wiley, Chichester 1983.
Brodie, B. *Strategy in the Missile Age*. Princeton UP 1965.
Brodie, B. & F. M. *From Crossbow to H-Bomb* Indiana UP 1973.
Brookner, E. Phased-array radars. *Scientific American*, February 1985.
Builder, C. H. *Non-nuclear Means for Strategic Conflict*. IISS, Adelphi Paper 200, London 1985.
Bush, V. *Modern Arms and Free Men*. Simon & Schuster, NY 1949.
Calder, N. *Nuclear Nightmare*. BBC, London 1979.
Calder, N. (ed.) *Unless Peace Comes*. Viking, NY 1968.
Campbell, C. *War Facts Now*. Fontana, London 1982.
Canby, S. Military reform and the art of war. *Survival*, May/June 1983.
Chant, C. & Hogg, I. *The Nuclear War File*. Ebury, London 1983.
Chou, T.-W. Composites. *Scientific American*. October 1986.
Cockburn, A. *The Threat*. Random House, NY 1983.
Collins, J. M. *US-Soviet Military Balance*. CRS, Washington 1984.
Craxton, R. S. Progress in laser fusion. *Scientific American*, August 1986.
Curran, S. & Curnow, R. *The Penguin Computing Book*. Penguin, London 1983.
Dando, M. & Rogers, P. *The Death of Deterrence*. CND, London 1984.
David, P. *Star Wars and Arms Control*. Council for Arms Control, London 1985.
Dean, D. J. *Low-Intensity Conflict and Modern Technology*. Air University Press, Alabama 1986.
Douhet, G. *The Command of the Air*. Office of Air Force History, Washington 1983.
Dunnigan, J. F. *How to Make War*. Arms & Armour, London 1982.
Dupuy, T. N. *Numbers, Predictions and War*. Macdonald & Jane's, London 1979.
ESECS. *Strengthening Conventional Deterrence*. Macmillan, London 1983.
Feuchtwanger, E. J. & Mason, R. A. *Air Power in the Next Generation*. Macmillan, London 1979.
Fox, G. C. & Messina, P. C. Advanced computer architectures. *Scientific American*, October 1987.
Freedman, L. *Strategic Defence in the Nuclear Age*. IISS, Adelphi Paper 224, London 1987.
Freedman, L. *The Evolution of Nuclear Strategy*. Macmillan, London 1981.

Frisch, O. R. *The Nature of Matter*. Thames & Hudson, London 1972.
Garden, T. *Can Deterrence Last?* Buchan & Enright, London 1984.
Geissler, E. (ed.). *Biological and Toxin Weapons Today*. SIPRI, Stockholm 1986.
Gottemoeller, R. E. *Land-attack Cruise Missiles*. IISS, Adelphi Paper 226, London 1987.
Graham, D. O. *The Non-Nuclear Defense of Cities*. Abt, Cambridge Mass. 1983.
Gray, C. S. *American Military Space Policy*. Abt, Cambridge Mass. 1982.
Gray, C. S. & Meyer, S. M. The military uses of space. *Survival*, September/October 1983.
Griffiths, F. & Polanyi, J. C. (ed.) *The Dangers of Nuclear War*. Toronto UP, 1979.
Harding, D. (ed.) *Weapons*. Galley Press, London 1984.
Harris, C. J. & White, I. *Advances in C3 Systems*. Peregrinus, London 1987.
Hedges, R. L. *Computer Science: Training in the DOD*. NDU, Washington 1983.
Higham, R. *Air Power*. St Martin's Press, NY 1972.
Hill-Norton, P. *Sea Power*. Faber, London 1982.
Hillis, W. D. The connection machine. *Scientific American*, June 1987.
Hockaday, A. *The Strategic Defence Initiative*. CCADD, London 1985.
Holley, I. B. *Ideas and Weapons*. Yale UP, 1953.
Howe, R. W. *Weapons*. Abacus, London 1981.
Hurley, A. F. *Billy Mitchell: Crusader for Air Power*. Bloomington 1975.
IISS. *New Technology and Western Security Policy*. Adelphi Papers 197–199. IISS, London 1985.
Jasani, B. *Space Weapons and International Security*. OUP, Oxford 1987.
Kallis, E. M. *Chemical Warfare*. CRS, Washington 1981.
Kaplan, F. M. Enhanced radiation weapons. *Scientific American*, May 1978.
Kear, B. H. Advanced metals. *Scientific American*, October 1986.
Kirby, S. & Robson, G. *The Militarisation of Space*. Wheatsheaf, London 1987.
Kumar, C. Strategic defense and DEW. *Scientific American*, September 1987.
Lee, C. *War in Space*. Hamilton, London 1986.
Lenat, D. B. Software for intelligent systems.*Scientific American*, September 1984.
Levine, R. D. Supercomputers. *Scientific American*, January 1982.
Mason, R. A. (ed.) *War in the Third Dimension*. Brassey's, London 1986.
Matisoo, J. The superconducting computer. *Scientific American*, May 1980.
Mayo, J. S. Materials for information and communication. *Scientific American*, October 1986.
Meselson, M. & Robinson, J. P. Chemical warfare & chemical disarmament. *Scientific American*, April 1980.
Pardoe, G. K. C. *The Future for Space Technology*. Pinter, London 1984.
Parmentola, J. & Tsipis, K. Particle beam weapons. *Scientific American*, April 1979.
Pierre, A. J. (ed.) *The Conventional Defense of Europe*. Council on Foreign Relations, NY 1986.
Prentis, S. *Biotechnology*. Orbis, London 1985.
Quigg, C. Elementary particles and forces. *Scientific American*, April 1985.
Ranft, B. (ed.) *From Ironclad to Trident*. Brassey's, London 1986.
Robinson, J. P. P. Chemical weapons and Europe. *Survival* January/February 1982.
Schawlow, A. L. Laser light. *Scientific American*, September 1968.
Schichlte, C. *The National Space Program*. NDU, Washington 1983.
Schroeer, D. *DEW and Strategic Defence: a Primer*. IISS, Adelphi Paper 221, London 1987.
Seagrave, S. *Yellow Rain*. Abacus, London 1982.
Simone, D. de. *The Effects of Nuclear War*. OTA, Congress 1980.
Sims, N. A. *Biological and Toxin Weapons*. Council for Arms Control, London 1986.
Smart, I. *Advanced Strategic Missiles*. IISS, Adelphi Paper 63, London 1969.
Snyder, C. *The Strategic Defense Debate*. Pennsylvania UP 1986.
Sorrels, C. A. *US Cruise Missile Programs*. Brassey's, London 1983.
Steiberg, M. A. Materials for aerospace. *Scientific American*, October 1986.
Strachan, H. *European Armies and the Conduct of War*. Allen & Unwin, London 1983.
Stringer, H. *Deterring Chemical Warfare*. Pergamon, Oxford 1986.
Tank, D. W. & Hopfield, J. J. Collective computation. *Scientific American*, December 1987.
Taylor, T. B. Third generation nuclear weapons. *Scientific American*, April 1987.
Terraine, J. *Right of the Line*. Hodder & Stoughton, London 1985.
Till, G. *Air Power and the Royal Navy*. Jane's, London 1979.
Till, G. (ed.). *Maritime Strategy and the Nuclear Age*. Macmillan, London 1982.

Tirman, J. *The Fallacy of Star Wars*. Random House 1984.
Tsang, W. T. The C3 laser. *Scientific American*, November 1984.
Tsipis, K. Laser weapons. *Scientific American*, December 1981.
Ulam, S. M. Computers. *Scientific American*, September 1964.
Vachon, G. K. Chemical weapons and the Third World. *Survival*, March/April 1984.
Van Allen, J. A. Space science. *Scientific American*. January 1986.
Wallin, L. B. (ed.) *Military Doctrines for Central Europe*. Swedish National Defence Research Institute, Stockholm 1986.
Wit, J. S. Advances in antisubmarine warfare. *Scientific American*, February 1981.
Wright, D. M. & Paszek, L. J. (eds.) *Science, Technology and Warfare*. USAF Academy 1969.
Yonas, G. Fusion power with particle beams. *Scientific American*, November 1978.

Index